Cry For Help

(Collection of Poems)

BHUPENDRA M. GANDHI

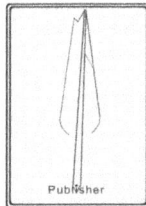

Publisher

MA PUBLISHER

Copyright © Bhupendra M. Gandhi 2019

Published by MA Publishing

Printed in United Kingdom

ISBN-13: 978-1-910499-49-8

Cover designed by Mayar Akash
Cover photo by Bhupendra M. Gandhi
Typeset in Times Roman

FSC
www.fsc.org
FSC® C004658

Paper printed on is FSC certified, lead-free, acid-free, buffered paper made from wood-based pulp. Our paper meets the ISO 9706 standard for permanent paper. As such, paper will last several hundred years when stored.

Acknowledgement

This is my fourth book, a collection of my poems; the first three were collection of short stories, mostly based on true life experiences of friends and family members, spiced up with a writer's imagination, as imagination is a fertile ground, it has no limit, no boundaries and certainly no restrictions.

Although I have already mentioned before in my acknowledgement, in my popular book "Ivory Tower" I would like to stress the help and encouragement I have received from Shri C. B. Patel, Editor and publisher of Asian Voice and Gujarat Samachar, the most widely read weekly newspapers outside India. He gave me the first break when I was entering the competitive world of journalism. Some of these poems were first published in Asian Voice, in "Poet's Corner".

Shri Krishan Raleigh is the Managing Director and Chief Editor of upmarket magazine "India Link" where I have my own column "From Far and Near" for the last twenty years. It is indeed a privilege and honour to write a regular column with complete freedom, in such a prestigious magazine.

My special thanks goes to Lord Dolar Popat, the pillar of the British Asian community who kindly wrote "Forward" for this book, dealing in detail my achievement and standing among the British Indian community. He is indeed "People's Lord" so easily approachable, always able and willing to help anyone who may approach him, need his help and advice.

I owe a debt of gratitude to my wife Kumudini who has stood-by me in my hour of need, especially when I had a mishap in NHS hospital, when a two hour stay in a "Day Ward" resulting in a twenty two night stay, fighting for my life. Kumudini, being a nurse by profession, was an added advantage.

Lastly but not least my MP Rt. Hon. Shri Barry Gardiner who was the first person I interviewed in my own home for India Link, just after he was elected for the first time and has stood by me in my hour of need, especially during my hospital mishap. He is more than my MP, a good friend.

As I had a very interesting and vivid life in Tanzania and later on here in London, I am tempted to write my biography but at my age, perhaps it is a "Bridge Too Far!"

I hope I will get as much support for this book as I have received for my writings in Asian Voice and India Link.

Forward

Poetry is one of the world's greatest treasures. It helps us to understand the significance of words themselves. Some of the World's greatest texts, like Ramayana and Mahabharata, as well as the works of William Shakespeare's are in poetry. By writing and reading poetry, one understands importance of every single word and their placement. It makes us see things in completely new light.

In an age where social media is booming and where we are deliberately using fewer words to express ourselves, we remain indebted to authors like Bhupendra Gandhi who help us appreciate and value the use of words through poetry.

The book is thought provoking and through insightful full collection of poems focusing on a range of topics, from loneliness, ethical values to environmentalism. Each time I read a poem, it brought out a new hidden meaning. Reading this collection of poems was a reminder to me of the importance of words in expressing ourselves. In the age of increasing global political and economic uncertainty, Bhupendra emphasises to readers how easy it is to be misunderstood, one of the primary reasons for disputes across the world today.

Throughout the collection of poems, you get an insight into Bhupendra's journey in life and core values of Britishness. Despite being an accountant by background, Bhupendra was never one for numbers. Born in Dar Es Salaam, Tanzania in 1938, a then British colony, Bhupendra grew up and was educated at a local English media school where he grasped his love for words and writing.

Bhupendra fondly remembers how his art for writing flourished during Princess Margaret's official Royal Visit to Dar Es Salaam in early fifties. It was then his teacher Mr I. K. Vyas asked his students to write an essay on Princess Margaret's visit. At the time Princess was an international style icon whose visit mesmerised the whole of East Africa.

Before starting his essay, Bhupendra asked Mr Vyas the word limit for the assignment. Mr Vyas advised that there is no formal word limit, given that no one had ever written more than 4 sides A5 book pages of 400 words or less before. To every one's surprise, Bhupendra wrote 50 pages, expertly written on Princess Margaret's visit. This was the incident Bhupendra's gift for writing was discovered and where he was encouraged to take up writing more seriously.

Bhupendra went on to write a number of short stories, poems and articles which were widely published in various publications in East Africa, as well as in India. Bhupendra came to London in February 1968, during the premiership of Labour

Prime Minister Harold Wilson, when James Callaghan was Home Secretary. He more or less made their cherished British passports redundant. Bhupendra would continue practicing as an accountant and did not take up writing again until early 1990 during his retirement.

Unfortunately, in 1999 Bhupendra underwent severe health complications when a simple liver biopsy by a junior doctor went terribly wrong, turning a two hour stay in a day ward became a 22 night struggle to survive, undergoing a major operation which affected his health and wellbeing. Feeling a mixture of pain, anger and despair, Bhupendra turned to writing, using his pen to express how he felt. Bhupendra has captured this incident vividly in his short story, "To Hell and Back."

He turned his life around and decided to take up writing full time. It was the first time in his life where he was able to fulfill his passion, despite his medical condition, poor health. He secured a regular column in Shri C. B. Patel's Asian Voice, the largest ethnic publication outside India. Not always the most popular columnist, Bhupendra fast became a well-respected and critical columnist who politicians like me feared not to get the wrong side of! Bhupendra also became a leading interviewer, covering Narendra Modi's visit to London in 2002 when he was CM of Gujarat and well-known British MP's like Barry Gardiner, Sarah Teather, Gareth Thomas and many more.

Bhupendra then took-up writing novels; his popular novels include Ivory Tower and Olive Grove, a collection of short stories which include some of his short stories translated from Gujarati to English, changing background, location and characters to suit Western readers. At the age of 80, Bhupendra is still going strong and vows to write his autobiography, articulating his journey from Dar Es Salaam to post-Brexit UK and everything in between.

Bhupendra remains one of the most inspiring and respected writers within British Indian community. Through his collection of poems, you will grasp and catch glimpses of his struggle and despair, achievement and rewards, something we can all relate to. He is a proud British Indian who states that he would not be where he is today on literary front if it were not his British education in Tanzania. His British values of free speech, democracy, hard work and enterprise stayed with him in expressing his life through his writings.

I hope you enjoy reading this collection of poems as much as I did.

Lord Dolar Popat, May 2019

CONTENT

Rogue Elephant

Alone alone, lonely, spurned by one and all
On this wild beautiful ever green meadow
This vast, empty, yet alive open land
In the middle of wild African heartland

We call it unique, unmatched Serengeti Plain
So serene, so beautiful, yet so fulfilling
No wonder it is love at first sight
Heaven on earth, a sweet home to millions

A land of glory for many of nature's creation
I was born on this heaven on earth
Not so tine a baby, in an elephant heard
A gathering of loving, caring elephants

It was a congregation of some thirty and three
Small and large, young and elderly
Weak and strong, suckling and grown
A picture of health, happy and in herd

A real family, a contended assembly
My early life, my childhood prime
So lovingly spent, on this Serengeti Plain
Soon I grew up, into a strong, healthy bull

My advent of youth, my prime of life
Made me adventurous, challenging the pride
The heard is always led from the front
By a strong and healthy bull impudence

His reign is supreme, a master of herd
Guarding his harem with all his might
Strict disciplinarian, youngsters abide
His rule supreme, keeps everyone in line

Advent of youth, basic desire of life
Soon turn young bull ambitious, battle primed
Even if the coast may be too high
He could not help, nature's desire

This is law of Mother Nature, everyone abide
No escape, heart filled with actuate desire
Young and foolish, adventure inevitable
No matter what the end may be

Challenge inevitable, battleground selected
Young bull, the pride of his generation
Gauntlet thrown, seconds announced
Challenge propelled, willingly accepted

Soon giant bulls in their prime, fight for survival
The winner to be crowned a king for life
His reign supreme, his harem preserved
It is a fight for life, faint heart won't survive

The ground shakes, hurricane strikes
Earthquake in the making, dust cloud rise
Trumpeting sound awaken one and all
The burial ground gives up its dead

Sunrise masked with dust-bowl, sunset arrive
At last the battle is over, winner crowned
The loser retreat to live a solitary, wondering life
Young bull, a life in prime, defeated and expelled

Nowhere to run, nowhere to go, homeless and alone
Turning the young, prudent bull an inevitable **Rogue**
The long, fulfilling, promised life, nearing the end
What a tragedy to fall on such a noble animal!

****

Cry For Help

I saw a shoal of whales
Small and large, happy and content
Swimming in the mass of ocean waters
As free and happy as could be

One of them, the leader of the shoal
Swam out to me and said
Hi! My friend, can I speak to thee
Please lend me thy ear, for I may not be here

Humans are supposed to be considerate and clever
God made you supreme to be our guardian angel
Then why you act like teenage thugs
Like a bull in a china shop!

You make our lives a living hell
Look at my family, some twenty and two
Young and old, suckling and strong
A picture of health, happy and content

No worry, no enemy in our ocean paradise
Bar greedy humans, the ultimate parasite
I am afraid I will be caught one day
A big, powerful harpoon, all steel sharp and solid

Fired from a Japanese or a Norwegian whaler
Will explode on impact, killing me outright
My heart torn to pieces, destroying my soul
A river of blood will pollute thy ocean

A lingering death, undignified end for noble creature
My lifespan, one hundred years of joy and fun
Roaming the wild, foaming seas, visiting the poles
Reduced to no more than twenty and two

Ducking and diving, dodging harpoon, having no respite
Are we having fun, you must be joking!
It's a struggle for survival for us all
Taking each day as it comes, at a time

What have we done to offend thee industrious humans
That you want to hunt us till obliteration
Rubbing the salt in our painful wounds
Calling the cull a research science!

Ending on your dinner plate, a cruel mystifying pleasure
I fail to understand why your stomachs do not churn
At the sight of the slaughter of the innocent
To feed your young, on flesh and blood

I have only one message for thee greedy, cruel humans
Leave us alone with Mother Nature
So that we could relax and have some fun
Spend some time with our family and Mother Nature

Our family needs respite from human excesses
Hopefully a long, happy and fulfilling life
If we become extinct, it will be a tragedy
An irreplaceable loss to a greedy mankind

Your children and grandchildren will be losers
Who will never see a spouting spectacle?
An unrivalled magic show, a spectacle supreme
On the vast, unending ocean stage

This is our gift to you, the undeserving humans
And to this beautiful green green planet Earth
That sustains us all, since time memorable
Sadly we will no more be able to call our Mother Earth.

****

Magnificent Albatross

Magnificent Albatross, king of the sky
Nature's creation delight

Albatross rule sky with unimaginable ease
Star of Southern hemisphere

Rarely sighted in the Northern hemisphere
South Atlantic his precious abode

Giving preference to Southern hemisphere,
As their sole abode no matter what

May need super brain to figure it out at all
Riding the wind, climbing the sky

With such an ease, roaming mighty oceans
Searching for partner for eternal life,

In the beautiful, light blue, high majestic sky
His body and soul, tossed up and down

In fierce gale that abounds Southern hemisphere
His nesting site not so easy to find

Albatross, undisputed king of the vast sky,
Blessed with eight feet of wing span

That could keep him afloat indefinitely
In comfort, with ease and grace

Flies effortlessly, without flipping its' wings,
Eats, rests and goes to sleep

On wings and wind, high in the Southern sky
A unique, mysterious bird,

Nature's wonderful creation to delight tired mind
But why, for what reason

He avoids vast, open never ending Northern sky
That could be his home

His kingdom, his domain, his precious paradise
Northern Hemisphere with more land-mass

Vast, mighty Atlantic and Pacific Oceans galore
No shortage of remote corners

Albatross painstakingly builds a nest, vast and specious
Indeed a well-furnished shelter

On remote, beautiful, isolated Isle de San Andres
A heaven on the ocean floor

His efforts, his hard work wasted without a partner
To share his dream paradise

His big mistake was to choose wrong, remote site
He went after isolation

Remoteness, nature's beauty in a safe heavenly place
No matter how far or lonely

His heavenly paradise abode it may have to be
Distant no obstacle with supper wings!

His score of some two decades and three
Being lonely and miserable

Is about to come to an abrupt end, with a gift of nature
Flew in an angel, to his delight

From the vast clear blue not so alien a southern sky
Female Albatross, beauty in making

Ugly duckling maturing into nature's beautiful swan
In this case it is Albatross

His luck has changed at last with nature's blessings
That no one can deny

Unique combination of sugar and spice came to light
To share his vast and spacious delight!

Lay some eggs, so as to continue his noble race
A family of four or six

Spreading unabridged delight to ease the mind
Survival of his gens

His heritage not in doubt when eggs are hatched
To every one's delight

Brought in the world not so tiny delightful chicks
His life mission accomplished

He can now spend, enjoy rest of his remaining life
In the company of his new found love

A Turkish delight with heavenly bright light
Where Sun is always on the horizon

With the blessings of God, a supreme creation
Hopefully life will be bed of roses

To eat, rest and play with his delightful siblings
In nature's paradise with God's blessings!

****

Ancient Land of Bharat

Bharat, ancient land of sage, sadhu and sanscruti
Much appreciated name of mighty nation

Land of learned Gurus, deities, temples and culture
Land with coastal beauty on Bay of Bengal

Not forgetting frothing, overflowing Arabian Sea
Where waters of holy rivers flows

Enriching the surrounding lands of natural beauty
Rivers Yamuna, Sarasvati, Brahmaputra,

Godavari, Krishna, Khavari, Narmada and Sutlej
Not forgetting holy Mother Ganga

Cradle of early civilization, bread basket for the nation
This is tip of iceberg when praising India

Haunting, bewitching beauty, culture of ancient India
Where Himalayas kiss the sky

Not forgetting Western Ghat Mountains of the South
That makes Kerala Venice of India

Granary of ancient world, keeping hunger, famine at bay
Feeding civilized world with grain galore!

Bharat, Center of civilization, learning universities galore
Teaching weaponry, medicine and astrology

Not forgetting agriculture, architect and economics
Well-known universities include Takshashila,

Nalanda and Valabhi, Vikramshila, Banaras and Varanasi
A few amongst many, bastion of learning

Most famous Sandipani, source of Lord Krishna's wisdom
Where Lord Krishna spent his childhood

Lifelong friendship between Prince Krishna, Pauper Sudama
Lasted well into adulthood, never forgotten

Pauper Sudama rewarded with life of luxury, spiritual blessings
Fulfillment, at nod of Lord Krishna's blessings

Noble land of Bharat, birth place of Lord Rama, Lord Krishna
Not forgetting Mahavir, Buddha and Guru Nanak

That gave the world noble religions galore, Hinduism taking lead
Followed by Buddhism, Jainism and Sikhism

Gave birth to great ancient kingdoms, Maurya and Gupta dynasty
Chandragupta, an untouchable boy

A warrior king supreme, under guidance of Guru Vishnu Gupta
Popularly known as Chanakya

Liberated, united Bharat, from the remnants of Alexander the Great
Establishing the Maurya dynasty

With unparalleled skill and wisdom of the ancient land of Bharat
Ruling the land from Kabul to Kanyakumari

Chandragupta followed by son Bindusara, grandson Ashok the Great
The world has never seen such a noble

Wise and learned Emperor in the making, in the mould of Ashok
Warrior king turned pacifist

After watching carnage at Orissa battlefield, killing thousands
Embraced Buddhism, the noble culture

Sending his ambassador of peace far afield to China and Japan
Converting the entire ancient world

To the supreme ideology of noble Lord Buddha, the saviour
Empires come and go, even mighty Roman,

Greek and British Empire, where Sun never set, did not last long
But peaceful religions, cultural superiority

Goodwill and milk of human kindness, generosity will never weather
Last until human existence no more

Nobel Gandhi, inventor of Satyagrah, peaceful disobedience
Nelson Mandela, following into Gandhi's footsteps,

Liberating South Africa from egoistic white euphemists
Racial segregation that enslaved humanity

Different era, different age, discrimination was wide spread
On racial, religion, cultural or political

Any excuse, under uncomfortable Jim Crow's law in America
Who can forget "I have a dream" speech!

Words uttered from mouth of Martin Luther King Junior!
Gandhi and King, sacrificed their lives

In the service of humanity, to give us all equality
Never forger, their sacrifice

That made our world a much better place for one and all
Where children live with pride and freedom.

Never forget the sacrifice of these noble, valued humans
Who laid their lives, so that we have freedom!

****

Anger

I seem to be angry all the time
For what reason, I don't know why
It makes me miserable, sad and jumpy
Worse, I take it out, on nearest and dearest

On people I love most, people I admire
That is on my sweet innocent mum
And my best friend, Henry the dog
The lifelong faithful companion

How can I get rid of my sticky companion!
An uninvited, unwelcome guest
Who sticks to me like a louse!
Sucking my blood, a Dracula in the making

No matter how hard I try, keep the distance
It's always lurking in the background
Like a long sharp and clear shadow
Seen when it's bright and sunny

But always absent, nowhere to be seen
When it's dark and gloomy
A fair weather friend, a one way traffic
Who takes a lot, by any means!

Fair or foul, right or wrong, just or nauseating
But fails to give anything in return
Except misery and broken heart
Pain and ache, throbbing and pang

But it all changed on one sunny summer's day
It was warm, bright and shinning
Birds were busy feeding their young
A sight for sore eyes, a delight of life

I was tending my garden, digging and weeding
When I heard a knock on my door
I will always remember, the jingle of the bell
The sweet, innocent gentle face

A face that can bring a smile, mend a broken heart
The sweet, innocent gentle and caring face
A face that can mellow my anger, my pain
Bring me out of depression and melancholia

I was greeted with a Lord's message
Jesus, Rama, Krishna are the Lords
A kind of guardian angel of my own
Who gave me hope, courage and valour!

My life was changed, nothing is the same
My anger is no more, disappeared and gone
I was awaken from a bad dream
The nightmare gone with delight of dawn

Now my life is all sweet and mellow
An eternal bond, friendship with the Lord
That is the key for my glory and hope
I am a changed person, loved by all

So when you are passing through a bad time
Do not give up hope, faith and self-belief
Always remember, every cloud has silver lining
Rainbow has many unseen colours

These colours always hidden until the right moment
When rain and daylight combination prevails
A night is always followed by sunny dawn
Lord will look after you, if you don't give up hope.

****

Autumn Of Life [Arrive]

Trees are losing their foliage, chill in the air
Trees will look like skeletons, bones without flesh!
Streets covered with fallen, discarded leaves
All brown, wet and slippery, rotting in the air

The days are short; the sun is shy like a new bride
Warmth and sunshine in short supply
The darkness abounds, a nocturnal paradise
That drains spirit, make life a struggle to survive

The old and weak, shy and chatty, tiny and tall
A victim of gloomy weather and light famine
Afraid to go out where muggers abound
No one to turn to, care in short supply

New generation is different from trusted old one
The family ties do not have much accord
Live far and apart, out of sight, out of mind
Children hardly know their grandparents

Help and hope too far on the horizon, a silver lining
The arrival of Christmas brings a cheer and smile
On the old weather beaten face and lonely heart
A visit from the forgotten family and friends

Grand children bring a rare ray of hope and sunshine
Children's smile fills tired heart with pride and joy
For a while everything is fine, a real delight
No more loneliness or suffering in silence

The pleasure is guaranteed until the New Year's Day
But soon the fun and delight is no more with the old
Young ones fly off in different directions
The nest is deserted, loneliness is restored

Gloom and doom, despair and desperation is doubly strong
Snow falls in severe silence, turning home into prison
The land is white but sky is grey and extremely cold
The ray of hope is the noise of the children

Busy building a snowman with soft snow, carrot as a nose
Whoosh! flies a snowball past my window
Brings the sweet childhood memory flooding back
Those were the happy days, no worries in the air

When fun, family, love and respect was in abundance
No one was lonely; every one part of an extended family
No neglect of the weak and old, no confinement indoor
The art of talking, sitting together around a live fire

It was an enjoyment, a togetherness appreciated by all
Old and young, weak and strong, suckling and all
Streets were safe, grey hair, old age respected
Winkled skin, grey hair was part of culture and pride

The mugging of the weak and old was not yet invented
Old people's homes were not even on the drawing board
It was a caring, sharing society, one for all and all for one
No one was lonely, neglected or forgotten

It was a one big happy, united family, living under one roof
Every cloud had a silver lining, rainbow always on the horizon
Gloom, doom and lonely night was followed by a sunny dawn
How my heart yearn for good old carefree days

A word of wisdom from a forgotten, unremembered soul
Preserve the good old tested and tried ways of life
There is wisdom and experience in the old soul
For new is silver but old is irrepressible gold.

Live your life to the full, enjoy every God given moment
For time is short, happiness in short supply
Make the hay; enjoy life, while the sun shines
Call of Mother Nature will inevitably arrive

Dust to dust, ashes to ashes, that is law of Mother Nature
For one and all, rich and poor, exemption do not apply
So be prepared, be ready to depart for reunion
With kind and caring Mother Nature.

****

Crocodile Tears

Crocodiles, the relics of the past
Remnants of prehistoric era

Even when dinosaurs ruled the world
Mighty dinosaurs perished

Cunning Crocodiles did not only survived
They thrived and multiplied

Crocodiles rule rivers, even mighty seas
Where they are undisputed kings

Crocodiles, like fish, do not shed tears
Shedding tears is alien to its nature

So why we say these are crocodile's tears
Is it an expression to tease humans!

Comparing our existence, our selfishness
With wild, cruel, cunning crocodiles

Who prey on land animals like zebras, deer!
Their favourite prey is wilder beast

Even baby elephants, pigs and humans
Whoever goes near water's edge!

To drink, to refresh, extinguish their thirst
Necessary evil in hot mid-day sun

It is a slow, painful, cruel death by drowning
Then it is essential for their survival

By any means, fair or foul, by hooks or crooks
That is why crocodiles are so feared

Crocodiles have no scrupulous, no ethics
Their aim is to survive, multiply

Crocodiles will always be here, come what may
Even when mighty human race no more

Obliterated, gone for good, in dinosaurs style
It is the human act of madness

Developing weapons of mass destruction brought
Human civilization to an early end

Civilization that existed since time memorable
Will come to unimaginable end!

Whose fault supreme humans are no more!
On this habitable planet earth!

Eradicated by greed, pushing nuclear button!
That created hell of fire

Unimaginable nuclear pollution that devours all
Impossible for anyone to survive

This man made holocaust of sheer hell!
Why humans the super race

Ultimate gift from God to Mother Earth!
Don't learn from past mistakes

Live in peace and harmony, enjoy life
A gift from all mighty God

Enjoy, rock around the clock till day light!
For human life is one off

A precious, ultimate gift, not to be wasted
Enjoy it from cradle to grave!

****

Day Dreaming

I thought I won a jackpot on national lottery
But in reality, I was day dreaming

It is good pass-time, when you are short on luck
Emotions flowing on top of the cloud

Music flowing, melody capturing confused mind
Rhythmic music, soul searching lyrics

Full Moon shines long and bright, on cloudless sky
Filled with sweet smell of roses by night

Mellowed moonshine in the middle of silent night
Do not go to sleep when Moon is in sight

Watching waves, playing with Moon light bright
Appearing, disappearing, in full Moon tide

Waves, high and low, rise, retreat, in nick of time
Mellowed sound in Moon lit night

Rags to riches, in the land of midnight Moon!
Competing with Sun, still in the sky

From cradle to grave, come what may in nutshell
London Bridge is falling down

Every cloud has silver lining, so don't lose hope
Grass always green in neighbour's garden

Grass root beauty, desert bloom, simmering with fury
Make hay while the Sun shines

Navigate the earth, but no place like sweet home,
Home is where your heart flutters

Mother Nature, kind, caring, full of promise galore
You know you are in good company

Eternal peace, freed from the circle of birth and death
Reunion with Mother Nature, in nick of time!

****

Decision Time

The time has come to make a decision
How to spend the millions I so deservedly won
On our National Lottery that's punters delight

My luck so dormant, for a very long time
Suddenly came alive, to my delight never knew why
Perhaps a test for my dedication and determination

My bank manager, whom I could not recall by name
A stranger whom I had to approach with misgiving
Became a friend, calling me by my first name

Oh! What to do with my millions, lying dormant
Could I go to the moon and never come back
Or feed the starving millions who populate the land

What about our luckless cardboard city dwellers
Who sleep and shiver in doorways with guilt and shame
Old, sick and infirm, weak and fragile, ready to die

Who throng overburdened National Health Service!
I was told in childhood, charity begins at home
So it is my duty, obligation to look after my own

My story is that of rags to riches, with a stroke of luck
Changing a pauper into Prince Over-night
With the blessings of my beloved Lord Krishna

Friends and relations, schoolmates and colleague
Why not computers, Tablets and modern technology
To my old school and educational establishment

For friends and relations, relieve burden of home loans
Borrowings from sharks and mortgage repayments
Buy a bungalow, in a leafy, sleepy suburb

In rural, peaceful, prosperous area for my mum and dad
Who cared, nurtured me throughout my young life
It is time for obligation, payback with delight

Why not charter a cruise liner named Queen Elizabeth Two
To sample delight of world cruse for near and dear
That should be my obligation for one and all

Visiting faraway places of the unexplored world
Bali, Sumatra, Mauritius and Hawaii
Not forgetting attractions of our own

On our door-step, lies beautiful Madera, lonesome Formentera
The place where Jules Verne wrote his best novels
Twenty thousand league under the sea

My favourite character, Captain Nemo, so wise and determined
Commander of unsinkable submarine named Nautilus
Determined to save world from wars and starvation

An idealistic character, who won our hearts and minds
The novel, the story made popular by Hollywood
Embodied name Jules Verne in literary history

Well, you must have guessed, no win, no money galore
Just day dreaming, no harm in fantasising
What may one day become a reality?

It is better to live in hope, happiness and expectation
Than to be miserable, sulking all the time
Life is short, so make hay while sun shines!

****

Emptiness

Life is like a sweet dream
Wake up and it's gone

It's a shadow, fall darkness
Nowhere to be seen

It belongs in ever perpetually
To the mighty Sun God

The shadow is not mine or yours
It has no permanent home

When the Moon is in full bloom
Shadows may follow

All the time, from noon to night
It will never fade

When Sun is bright, high in sky
Until sun sets in western sky

That's why I feel it's time to go
Know not my destination

Nor my journey route that matters most
How can I plan ahead!

When you are gone, leaving me alone
Life is a mirage

An oasis of hope, happiness and pleasure
All in anticipation!

A dream, happy world forever for lost soul!
Ended before it's even born!

End of hope and dream, no more than mirage!
My life is empty shell

Forever unfulfilled, never reached the top
Life is smouldering fire

Gone up in smoke, leaving me all alone
Soul will wander no more

When I am for-ever gone like a shadow
With the demise of the Sun

God, give me strength to say goodbye
To one and all, every soul

Especially my lovely mum, as good as gold!
Not with heavy heart

But a smile and a cheer deep in my heart
When the time is right

Departure will no more in any doubt in my mind
Reunion assured, with Mother Nature.

****

Failure

Failure is a two edge sword,
Sharp and spiky

That brings on melancholy sadness
Failure sinks my heart,

Filled with sorrow in sea of sadness
Without a ray of hope

Every act brings on counter reaction,
Pain, agony gains upper hand

Try to hide my pain, failure and anxiety
Without much success

Devoid of hope or ray of sunshine
This is time to groom friends

Those who are tried and tested friends
Will stand solid next to you

Others, opportunist, fair weather friends
Nowhere to be seen

In your hour of need, in time of necessity
Shines like black-hole Star

That is true friendship, never in doubt
Heaven and hell is here on earth

Friendship bounds us from cradle to grave
Tried and tested in adverse time!

Test resolutions, determination with care
Warm-hearted consideration

Help, kindness will alleviate the pain
Setbacks, like a pain and failure

Always come and go without a trace!
Every cloud has silver lining,

In time of rainy, damp, depressing days
So do not ever lose hope

At the temporary loss of sunshine bright
So cheer up, smile once more

Live in ever enhancing expectation and hope
Happiness is on the horizon after all!

****

Friendship Betrayal

Without good friends, life becomes a drag,
Shallow and boring to no end!

Loyal friends are indeed sweet nectar of life
Sweet, kind and caring to the end!

Friends are loyal, stand by us in our hour of need
That is why friends are rated so high

If friend betrays, that is like Brutus's deep stab
On brave and trusting Julius Caesar

Betrayal of friendship, deep wounds difficult to heal
Broken promises lead to moral decline!

That begs the question why only I hung out to dry!
Hope to find the answer any time

Perhaps knowing truth may be worse than ignorance
Why did I loyally stood by her all these time

It was like a glass shattering into million tiny pieces,
Most hurting but unseen by human eyes

But it is not the right time, to wallow in self-pity
Did she knew I have feelings

My heart bleeds, life becomes misery, in moral decline
After all I am kind and caring human being

Friendship meant for life, stood by each other in time
Of real happiness, unimaginable strife

Loyal friends are so thin on surface, difficult to find
Unless you have Lord Krishna's blessings

Friendship and respect between Prince and Pauper
Is the shining, living example

Of true friendship between two unequal human beings
Lord Krishna had not an ounce of pride

Always loyal to his friends, devotees and man-kind
That's why Hare Krishna praised world wide

Lord Krishna gives us courage to be decent human being
To look at the world through rose tinted glasses

I tried not to let her win, get to me, using every means
At my disposal, but I have feelings

I am a decent, principled, kind and caring human being
Now I feel angry, heart filled with hatred

Seeking revenge, that makes me less of a human being
Oh God, do not fill my heart with anger

Hatred, with punishment in mind, one bad act, a betrayal
One act of foolishness on part of my sweetheart

Should not lead to judgment on every human kind
World is home to noble, courageous people

Lord Jesus Christ, Krishna, Buddha and Guru Nanak
God sent them down to Mother Earth

To test our resolve, character, reservoir of human milk
Of kindness, not human greed

When we feel who needs an enemy with friends like her
Do not despair; just give some time

Believe in yourself, never lose faith or patience
A time will come, wounds will heal

Nightmares will turn into sweet dreams, bed of roses
Without ups and down in life

Who will remember All Mighty who created us all!
Have to sleep often, on bed of nails

That's the test of God, to gauge us all in time of crisis!
So be patient, everything will turn to gold!

Life will again be sweet smelling roses, intended by nature
So relax, put your worries on back-burner!

Autumn Of Life

Trees are losing their foliage
Chill in the damp air

Soon trees will look like skeletons,
All branches, no leaves

Streets covered with discarded leaves
All brown, wet and slippery

Rotting in the cold and damp air
The days are short

The sun is shy like a new bride
Warmth and sunshine

In a nut shell, in short supply,
The darkness abounds

Creating unique nocturnal paradise
That drains the spirit

Make my life not worth living
The old and weak

Shy, timid and small, tiny and tall
Victim of gloomy weather

Light famine, sun does not shine
Where muggers abound

No one to turn to, safety in short supply
Help and hope on horizon,

A silver lining, a distant mirage
The arrival of Christmas

Brings cheers, smile to golden hearts
On old weather beaten face

Lonely hearts no more in despair
A visit from family members

And long lost childhood friends
Grand children galore

Bring rare ray of hope and sunshine
Children's smiles fill tired hearts

With enviable pride, joy and delight
For a while life is fine

A real Turkish delight to enjoy life
No more loneliness

Suffering in silence, no one to talk to
The pleasure is guaranteed

At least until New Year's Day
But soon fun and delight

Will disappear as fast as it came
Life no more fun and joy

Young ones fly off in different directions
Nest deserted, loneliness restored

Gloom and doom, despair and desperation
Loneliness is doubly strong

Snow falls day and night in severe silence
Turning home into prison

Land is white; sky is grey, extremely cold
Ray of hope no more

Sweet noise, mischievous laughter of children
Busy building a snowman

With red carrot as a nose on round face
Whoosh, flies a snowball

Bring childhood memory flooding back
Those were happy days

No worries, nor loneliness at home
It was a fun filled time

Family, love and respect in abundance
Happy home for one and all

Everyone part of an extended family
No neglect of weak and old

Nor neglect, confinement on your own
The art of talking

Sitting together around a live fire
Talking, laughing together

Not glued in front of TV, in one room
With gloomy, deadly silence

At least at dinner time, family unite
In chatty delight

Bonding unity, one for all, all for one
Never to be divided

Nor would greed take an upper hand
It was an enjoyment

Togetherness appreciated by one and all
Old, young, weak and strong

Suckling babies and matured adults
Streets were safe

Grey hair, ripe old age respected
Winkle skin, memory loss

Was part growing old, cultural pride
Mugging of the weak

Was not yet invented, nor on horizon
Old people's care-homes

Were not even on the drawing board
It was caring, sharing society,

One for all and all for one was the moto
The name of the game

No one was lonely, depressed or forgotten
Every one taken care of

It was a one big happy united family
In love and full of fun

Every cloud had a silver lining
Rainbow on the horizon

Gloom, melancholy and lonely night
Was followed by sunny dawn

How my heart yearn for good old days
A word of wisdom

From a forgotten, unremembered soul
Preserve good old days

Tried and tested ways of long life
There is much wisdom

Some experience in old soul well respected
For new is silver

But old is irrepressible, tried, tested gold
To be treasured forever.

****

Glory Of Bygone Days

I remain here in a sombre,
Gloomy, dark and desolate place

Isolated, alone, put to rest
Well over one hundred years ago

Neglected, covered with pest,
Unattended, overgrown with weeds

Yet I once lived a pleasant life,
Full of ups and down, zest and zeal

Person of charm, respect, wealth
Integrity, influence beyond question

Someone to look up to, for guidance, help
But it all came to nothing, abrupt end

A sudden, unexpected, gruesome end,
Suddenly, unexpectedly as I came and went

Remember me with some affection
As you pass by my grave, on summer's day

I was once, a rising star, well respected
In fact what you are to-day, sought after person

Healthy, wealthy, rich and wise
Cheery, famous, brave, loved, a family man

People called me "Alexander the Great"
A soul respected and admired in equal measure

Pillar of society, king of the ancient world
VIP in making, bud about to blossom

In Garden of Eden with Eve in attendance
Gift to mankind, that what I thought

Do not forget, keep embodied, in time,
You will be one day, what I am today

A forgotten soul lost in a human made maze o
Entombed in expensive sandalwood coffin

Silk-lined coffin, soft and comfy but forgotten by all
This is way of nature, here today, gone tomorrow

Out of sight, out of mind, never to be seen again
Sunk like Titanic, in cold Atlantic water

Make the hay while the sun shines bright and high
In pleasant blue, bright, sunny sky

Good deeds never go unrewarded for one and all
In the mighty kingdom of Supreme nature!

That is the unwritten law of sensitive nature
In God's magnificent manifesto

In wonderful, carefree world created for humans
A mighty God's creation for one and all

Be ready for unexpected, uninvited departure
Before the sky laden with dark

Menacing clouds of gloom, doom and misery!
All too familiar, descending on us

From thundering rainy, grey and cloudy sky
To reunite us with Mother Nature

Quick, unexpected end, charted by Mother Nature
The end that justifies the means

Written in our fate, even before we were born
Birth is a happy occasion

A gift from God, when everyone shed tears
Of delight and uncontrolled joy

Except the new born tiny baby who would cry
When my time has run out

Put me to rest in coffin of sandalwood, my choice!
Friends and family would shed tears

While I depart with a smile, having done my duty!
A fitting end to a courageous life

Hopefully appreciated, remembered by one and all!
With appreciation and heart of gold!

****

Harvest Festival

Harvest time, a wonderful occasion of the year
Fields over-laden with wheat and barley

Do not forget millet, corn and especially rice
That feeds both human and animals alike

To farmers' delight, fields are ready to harvest
With help of every family member

Small, young and grown-up, male and female
Children and adults, weak and strong

Harvesting is hard, back-breaking but rewarding work
Enjoy the fresh air and music of wild birds

Participation unconditional, enjoyment unlimited
Pick your own; eat to your heart's delight

That is quantum improvement in one's life enjoyment
Grab the opportunity without a second thought!

Need wheelbarrow for corn, potatoes and cassava
If you are picking the lot for winter survival

Have no worry; help is here, fill your baskets,
For every one and all

Ask for recipe, to turn glut of strawberry into jam
That keeps fresh all year round

Strawberries are every one's favourite, sweet and juicy
Eat with fresh cream to your heart's delight

Raspberry not so sweet, eat with cream and honey
To dim sweet, bitter taste not so good

But all fruits are not the same, nor are human taste
Every one's favourite, ripe and juicy mangoes

While watching Wimbledon, reminds onset of summer
Long, bright days and midnight Sun!

Sweet dreams, grain galore, soon ready for harvest
Filling silos with wheat and corn

Preparation for winter, saving for rainy days,
That's survival, name of the game!

Harvest time is festive time, with enjoyment galore
"Navratri" festival of nine days

Of dance and song, a festival for young and old
Enjoyed by one and all

Festival in temples, community halls and street corners
As well as on roof-tops!

This is special time of the year, not repeated for twelve months
To thank "All Mighty" for his blessings and food galore!

****

Ingenuity of Human Mind

Human beings are great creation of nature in time of delight
Empowered with noble, invincible, inventive mind
To serve us, the humanity at large

With inquisitive, supreme mind, cleverly hidden immorality
Tried to enslave their fellow human kind
To create a life of luxury and pride

For few, perceived, privileged tribes, who ruled supreme at the time
Aryans, Vikings, Dorians, Celtic and Mongols, name but few
Led by Mongol Kublai Khan and Alexander the Great

But human beings in their self-belief and extreme pride and prejudice
Forgot God and acted with cruelty and diseased mind
Bringing untold barbarism to civilized society

Shackled and enslaved their fellow human kind with extreme violence
Ever subservience to their cruel masters' unhinged delight
Denigration of human mind, not for the first time

Looted noble Mother Nature of all her hidden natural treasure
Makes it difficult to trust human's deceiving mind
That uses clever mind to commit hideous crimes

Born free, born with hope, excitement and harmonious expectation
In the vain hope of happiness, nurturing Mother Nature
It is time to liberate mind from human greed

In words of noble Mahatma Gandhi, there is enough for human need
But not for every, tiny insatiable human greed
That leads to ultimate human downfall

Use your unshackled mind to climb the ladder that brings pleasure
Make the mind supreme to liberate greedy man-kind
To create heaven on our beloved Mother Earth

Roman Empire, confluence of slavery, freedom and democracy
Could not indefinitely survive the onslaught
That led to the liberation of man kind

Gifted with noble thoughts, for the liberation of humanity at large
Peace, progress, happiness and family life always in sight
That gave birth to great saints and sages in time

Lord Jesus, Lord Rama, Lord Krishna, Buddha and saviour Guru Nanak
Descended from heaven on Mother Earth in the nick of time
To stop the deterioration, destruction of man kind

Human are like "Pied Piper" that bewitch, enslave their fellow tribe
To use and exploit their own for their personal gain
Exploiting weakness with ease and efficiency

Fertile, inquisitive, unbridled mind is behind every success in life
Stops the human misfortune that may fall on man-kind
All is well if the end justifies the means!

****

Lady Diana:
A People's Princess

Why, oh why you have to die so young, when in bloom
Leaving a bewildered nation behind, united in grief

There is a tear on every face, young and old, sick and robust
What about young Prince William and Harry

Why do they have to become motherless so young early in life
You were the queen of compassion, jewel in the Crown

A beacon of light and hope in the sea of despair and denigration
A true Princess, people's Princess, a friend in need

The world knows how some people who were so near and dear to you
Caused you pain, heartache and untold misery to you

Loneliness, not so pleasant or happiest of the abandoned childhood
Did not help you taking the first step to adulthood

No mother's love or a warm cuddle on a rainy stormy, lightening night
Black clouds in abundance, no silver lining or ray of sunshine

While the Rome burnt, your nearest and dearest Nero played fiddle
In the company of undesirable, without a care in the world

You stumbled alone with the love and support of your wonderful dad
Always in attendance, supporting your desire and destination

By grace of God, this ugly duckling turned into a beautiful, graceful swan
In the spring of adulthood, you met your charming Prince

Only turned out to be a nurtured carbon copy of a real gem in the Crown
No everlasting love or fulfilment, only sorrow and loneliness

Soon your married life became a web of deceit and pain, nothing gained
Deprived and dejected, harassed and humiliated

You sought comfort and consolation in the company of nearest and dearest
You opened your heart to a Knight in dashing armour

The Major turned out to be a minor, fake Knight of the "Round Table"
A hand grenade gift-wrapped as Christ present

That was the deep stab of Brutus on Julius Caesar, the betrayal most unkind
Heartbroken, felt abandoned, sought solace in charity work

The Royal exile, isolation unkind, soon turned out to be a blessing in disguise
She felt at ease in the world of sick, homeless and deprived

Serving the poor, lonely, abandoned and infirm became your life ambition
How well were you suited for a role of a guardian angel?

His Holiness the revered Pope residing in Rome and Archbishop of Canterbury
Not forgetting Mother Teresa, nor the jewel of Africa Nelson Mandela

These noble human beings, caring pillars of society, gave you seal of approval
This made you caring and brave, true friend of landmine rage

At last we thought you found true lifelong partner, knight in shining armour
He came and went in a flesh, before the eye can wink

Was it a dream, was it reality, lost in thoughts, you pinched in disbelief
How you wished it was a dream, not to be followed by nightmare

On a dark and gloomy, rain filled fateful night, in the heart of paradise Paris
All hell broke loose; accident round the corner, fury knew no bound

Now that the Princess is no more, who will comfort the sick, poor and old
Whom can we turn to in our hour of need and sorrow?

Can comfort ourselves your grave on **"Island of Hope"** will give us inspiration
Hope to light a candle in the memory of our beloved Princess

May her soul rest in eternal peace, free from pain, sorrow and betrayal
Diana, oh lovely, beautiful Diana, Queen of people's heart

Why you departed so soon when your presence, your charm and loving nature
So much in need, a Lady in the Lake, my heart goes to Thee.

****

Lion:
King of Jungle

Lion, a noble, courageous animal,
Undisputed king of the forest

A majestic beast of supreme Joy
Proud heritage, mane magnificent

Shining, fluttering in sunlight bright
Respected by one and all

Feared and respected, all at the same time
By jungle inhabitants, sharing habitat

Perched on a hill high, sitting in pride
Top of tallest landmark in sight

Keeping watchful eye, to every one's delight
A guardian angel, God sent delight

Free to roam the dense forest, his domain
Never kill just for momentary fun

That is why lion is respected, called the king
Lions are social animal, live in a harem

Bring up their young with pride and purpose
Taking care of young, weak and old

To every one's delight, the pride thrives
Enjoying the freedom of forest

Plenty of space to roam romantic wilderness
Hunt only when hunger strike

To feed, protect and safeguard the lion Pride
Lion-hearted is byword for courage

The word that describes the noble kings
Shivaji and Maha Rana Pratap

Brave kings of nobility, culture, patriotic pride
Who fight to protect the right!

To keep his kingdom safe, free from invaders
Who wants to loot and steal!

Milk the kingdom dry, devoid of humanity
Culture and culinary

As the Lion king grows old and weak,
As nature intended at the time

Inevitably could not rule supreme over the Pride
No longer enjoys the freedom

Of vast, great, green Serengeti wilderness
Challenge is inevitable

From young, ambitious pretender of the pride
No longer eat, sleep, play or rest

Peacefully, as intended, always on the guard
Come what may, pride prevails

The King will not relinquish his cherished harem
Fight to the end, die with dignity

Weak from hunger, as he could not chew food
With toothless mouth

Weak, old and handicapped, dejected by the Pride
It is time to say bond farewell

Either leave his beloved Pride or die with dignity
In a fierce, unwinnable fight,

Defeat in sight, kingdom lost, dies with knowledge
Knowing full well

That he leaves the Pride in safe and strong hand
What a tragic end for a noble beast

Who ruled supreme with dignity, until past his prime!
It is inevitable law of nature

Here today, gone tomorrow without a trace, forgotten by all
No matter what is the end!

The final destination reserved in heaven for the brave
Life may come to an abrupt end

But memories are preserved, deep in the unconscious mind
Shed no tears when I am gone

It is Kismat, written in one's nature when we are born
For ultimate reunion with Mother Nature!

****

Lonely Existence

Alone alone, all alone, in this wide wild world
Gone gone, my lifelong partner gone
After as association very very long
My early life, my childhood prime

Began on this most famous of all
A part of beautiful, swift flowing river Thames
A stretch of water, a tributary
More famously known as Henley Upon Thames

This beautiful, serene, peaceful, tranquil land
Henley regatta, a part of English social grace
A pride of place in the hearts and soul of all
Especially for sports mad, fun loving aristocrats

Born an ugly duckling, fate so cruel
Lost the love and protection, abandoned at birth
Yet passage of time, advent of youth
Soon turned you into prince charming

Favourite of all, young and not so old
Who stroll and wander along the river bank
In the long, long hours of the setting sun
The hazy days of summer warmth

On one early spring's dawn
When the sun was shining shy
Flew in from the clear blue sky
A young female, an angel in disguise

Soon she became a pride and joy
For swans residing on Henley Upon Thames
Call it Kismat, call it destiny, call it what you like
But for me, it was love at first sight

We soon got together, never separable
Made our home, our love nest in a swannery near by
We enjoyed each other, many summer together
Raising our young, our cygnets

We flew together, year after year
Before the onset of gloom and doom
You may like to call it a winter blue
To the promised land of ancient civilization

A land of milk and honey once
A land of sage and sanscruti Bharat
That gave us Lord Rama, Krishna and Nanak
A wonderland, a beautiful land

A land of tolerance for one and all civilization
We never fail to return to our land of birth and glory
We call it our homeland, our motherland
A land of fun, joy, enjoyment and fulfilment

The land we know it as Henley Upon Thames
Our joy was short lived, fun so cruelly curtailed
A poisonous bite, a dangling piece of lead
Dropped from an angler's tackle

Swallowed by my innocent angel
Led to my beloved's slow and painful death
It was the onset of autumn, winter not far away
Doom and gloom, all now too familiar

No more sunshine, flying, wondering together
No more escape from this gloomy weather
No more warmth or sunshine bright
No more visit to promise land of Israelite

Bharat, the land of sage, sanscruti and Mox
No more beauty of Kashmir, tranquillity of Kanya Kumari
Only the cold and damp of Henley Upon Thames
That is my winter prison, my all year home

This is the storey of my unfulfilled short life
The beginning of my painful and lonely existence
Now eagerly waiting for the call of nature
That will unite me with my darling and Mother Nature.

****

Swan is in many ways a unique bird. It is born as an ugly duckling. But soon turns into the most beautiful creation of nature. Swan mates, dare I say like a human being for life? So when one partner departs early, mainly due to human excesses, cruelty, knowing killed or unwittingly poisoned to death by pollution, a by-product of human excesses, the life of the remaining, surviving partner indeed becomes a lonely existence, hence this poem. I hope you will grasp the hidden message and enjoy reading this poem of my imagination.

The Long Journey

Childhood, my sweet, sweet childhood
Spring time, joy of eternal life

First step, tiny step on ladder to adulthood
Pure simple and innocent

Uncomplicated life till advent of adulthood
Seed germinating, bud blossoming

Petals opening, sweet smell freely flowing
From flowers sweet roses!

An apple in parent's eyes, mischievous
Yet deceptively innocent

No responsibilities in ever changing world
When under parents' umbrella!

As years go by, spring turns into summer
Childhood soon disappears

Matures into early unplanned adulthood
College sports and challenge

Advent of manhood, adventure galore
Go fast go straight

Nothing ventured nothing gained
Boon of life, pride of youth,

Desire of manhood, battle primed
Sweat and labour

Brings joy and pleasure in adult life
So sweet, surprisingly pleasant

Yet full of agony, surprise and rattle
Leads to a union of two souls

Two sweet and equally matching souls
This is the prime of life

No obstacles, happiness abounds
A family of one's own,

Until the young ones are fully grown
When they fly the nest

It is the beginning of the lonely life
The wisdom and experience

Of the inevitable approaching old age
The silver lining, the receding

Bald head providing mental maturity
Holding tightly to the memories

Of the bygone golden age of summer
Everything is be out of bound

Then comes old age and onset of winter
Gloom and doom in abundance

It's time for one or other to say farewell first
It brings on the isolation

Despair in old age, come journey's natural end
Eternal peace, reunion with Mother Nature

****

Ultimate Union

Marriage is a two way partnership
Grows deeper and stronger

As the time, days and years go by
So quick, so fast

It blossoms like a spring flower,
Early in young life

When family atmosphere is kind
Relation lovingly special

Togetherness, friendship, appreciation
In each and every way imaginable

All walk of life, inseparable and close
Ups and downs come and go

It is the love and the family bond
That unites, hold us together

Its romance, fantasy and excitement
That starts the marriage go round

But it's the addition of the new arrival
That truly unites, cements the bond

As the time go by, infants are no more
The nest-bound sprouts wings

Fly the nest, in search of pasture green
In the twilight zone of life

It is a testing time, for the weak and old
The relation knows no bounds

Companionship, loneliness rebounds
At the wrong time late in life

It mellows like mature wine, in long life
When at last one partner departs

Life for first time becomes burden too far
Old age, loneliness and frailty

Takes over life, unhappiness knows no bounds
It's time to take the stock

Of weeks, months and years gone by
Hoping the balance is right

It is the fervent wish of the other half
To travel together

On the last, final journey of no return
Never to be separated

No matter what, in life and death
That is the ultimate wish

Pray to All Mighty, for courage and wisdom.
On last, long, difficult journey

Where unknown obstacles abound all round
To the promised land of heaven.

Reunion with kind and caring Mother Nature
The ultimate destination forever!

****

Mother Nature

It is time to hail, praise and engages with caring Mother Nature
Who sustains and fulfils human life for ever
To the delight of planet Earth

Four seasons, as different as chalk and cheese, make the most of it
The long awaited spring brings joy and pleasure
No more cold, wet and winter gloom

Spring flowers abound, daffodils and tulip in bloom, roses in bud,
Cherry trees in blossom, carpeting the earth
With soft, sweet smelling petals

Winter cold, gloom and darkness gone, banished until next winter
It is time to make most of Mother Nature
Make the hay while the Sun shines

Follow the unique, sweet music of Pied Piper of summer delight
Children, play in park, make the noise to your hearts' delight
Schools closed, beginning of summer holidays

Then the advent of long awaited warm sunny days of summer
That brings in pleasure, with barbeque and picnic
Children's delight, to play and have fun

Drinks galore, food fit for the royal banquet in exotic surrounding
Friends and family, eager to eat, drink and be merry
For summer is here today, will be gone tomorrow

No schools, no more lessons, nor pressure of homework to submit
Fun all round, playing in park and in one's back-garden
Till parents come home, after a day's hard work

Kind but firm Mother Nature, full of wisdom, radiant and in prime
Hail thou spirit, emotions, faith in supreme Mother Nature
Though strength, wisdom and faith, human heritage

Sees us through in good time as well as when food is in short supply
So what! It is time to test one's trust in Mother Nature
She may be short of human needs at times

Fruits and berries, apples and pineapple, mango ripe in blazing sunshine
Feeds one and all, lion and lamb, no one left behind
Gradient Mother Nature, bless her mighty soul

Never worry, Mother Nature do not forget, always triumphs in the end
No matter what, come hell or high water, devil or deep blue sea
Survival of human kind is never in doubt

Pouring her kindness, looking after us, her blessings never in short supply
Thank All Mighty the Creator Supreme, for our good fortune
Without her mighty soul, our lives may not be sweet smelling

Hail our Mother Nature, her blessings makes life fertile and better
Without Mother Nature, life will be short, sharp and barren
So make the most, when the sun shines on Mother Nature.

****

My Wishes

I would like to see the world at peace
No hatred, no bloodshed, nor an upheaval

Could we ever achieve Ramrajya!
Kingdom with ultimate peace and prosperity

Or will it forever remain unfulfilled dream?
Until the day of our departure

Hope will always remain alive in our hearts
Sentiments will survive, no matter what!

It will slowly gain upper hand, to our delight
So never despair, good days are here

As we move into tomorrow's world with time
The past will become past

Not so irrelevant in the new upcoming world
A completely different game

Sun will shine brightly, banishing the gloomy clouds
Seven colours of rainbow will illuminate the sky

Filling our hearts and minds with hope and delight
Don't despair; happiness just round the corner

It is time to Rock around the Clock till midnight
Come what may, time to rise and shine

All you need is a bit of faith and trust in yourself
To take you to land of hope and glory!

****

Princess Diana:
Queen of our Heart

Princess Diana, Queen of our Heart, My heart goes to you
You were one in a million, a million to one for me!

Praised by everyone, poor, neglected, lonely and down trodden
Beacon of light and hope, sea of sorrow and despair

Yet deride by some, jealous and rumours of no consequence
At last when you seem to be settling down, in a dream home

With the love of your life and soul!
The fate so cruel, overtook the event

On the darkest of the dark night in romantic Paris
Your life so cruelly curtailed, dreams remain unfulfilled

You were gone in a flash that made us all helpless
No more cloud with a silver lining or a Knight in armour shinning
That sweet smiling face and heart of gold gone for ever

Although you are no more with us in flesh, in person
Your smiling personality and joyful nature

Will remain enshrined in our hearts for ever
Princess, our lovely, caring Princess, our hearts goes to Thee!

****

Shed The Darkness

Bring down the sectarian scrupulousness
Enlighten the mind, body will shine

Make it aware of shallow, fluctuating pride
That would not survive test of time

That fanaticism is number one enemy
Of unique God's creation mankind

That plunges humanity into unseen deprivation
Humans are supreme creation

To be guardian angel of all infant, adult life
Shed the falsehood, borrowed pride,

Welcome the truth, not falsehood of any kind
Lies never conquer hearts or minds

Be a guardian angel of the innocent,
Weak and strong, not so small

It is the law of nature, the fittest survive
The sun always shines

Bright and shiny, through the misty clouds
No matter how darken the sky is!

Every cloud has a kind of a silver lining
Of hope, faith and trust

That brings together humanity at large
The dark and cold night

Is always followed by dawn and warmth
No matter how long darkness shies

New bright, sunny day brings eternal hopes
Young ones have plenty of time

Their future is bright, under the cloudless sky
Grab opportunities, don't waste precious time!

The life of crime, may bring temporary relief
Success on the cheap never lasts long

Is no more than an illusion, a falsehood in disguise!
Never forget, life is a long journey,

Through rough and smooth, path so often blocked
We all have to pass through obstacles

No matter where we stand, how socially high
It is not the outwardly material wealth

That would survives, passage of tested time
Kindness, good deeds conquer

Our hearts and minds without a shred of doubt
It is in human nature to rise and shine

Come hell or high water, devil or the deep blue sea
No matter where one's heart and loyalty lies

Welcome truth, ultimate weapon of defence and victory
That could not be disguised by falsehood!

Eternal flame, salvation of soul, Mox and gutsy realisation
Will liberate the body, soul and mind

From the universal curse of vicious circle of birth and death
To eternal peace and liberation of soul.

****

Spring Time

Spring Time is here, somewhat late, but have no fear
Winter gloom is now a distant memory

Warmth and long summer sunshine reign supreme
Yellow daffodils and colourful tulips

Red Red Roses in bud, ready to bloom at any time
Spreading sweet smell all round

Birds are singing, fluttering their wings in spring air
Searching for suitable partners

Filling spring air with kind of perfume and excitement
With sweet smell of success!

Now I know, spring has arrived with all its splendour
Apple, pears and cherry trees

Covered all over in colourful white and pink blooms
Half open buds abound

Falling on the ground in not so gentle cool breeze
Carpeting Mother Earth

Soon it will be wonderful summer in its glorious prime
Children's favourite time

Schools are closed, no more homework to worry about
Heavenly holidays are here

It's time to play, relax and enjoy in the beautiful park
Have picnic, food and drinks galore

Plenty of food left to feed the birds residing in the pond
Take a walk in the open field

Look up at wondering, noisy sheep in large droves
Accompanied by new born cuddly lambs

Home grown strawberries galore, eat to your heart's delight
With sweeten thick fresh cream

Wait for heart beating; most popular tennis tournament is over
Glorious Wimbledon is here

Sport mad tennis enthusiasts, from every corner of the world
Queue up all day and night

In the hope of having the best Central Court seats available
For the start of Wimbledon tournament

To see their favourite home player one and only Andy Murray
Performing a miracle, in his prime

Winning the elusive Wimbledon prize, not once but twice
For the first time since Fred Perry

When our Fred Perry was in his prime, in mid thirties
Giving hope to tennis mad public

We have at last a player to cheer, Andy Murray is here
What a wonderful tournament

In it not daily event, for mighty Britain but millennium miracle
When a Brit player reign supreme!

****

Supreme Mind

Endowed with an invincible mind
Gifted with cognitive power

Created civilized society by any means
Wrested from nature all her treasure

Armed with famous loot mentality
Mind is a God given gift

Use it wisely, use it fairly, use it intelligently
Use it to benefit men kind

Humans are at the top of the league
Evolving at incredible speed

God made us powerful, supreme,
To take care of the weak

Those who are well down the league
Treasure nature's creation

God's gift to look after one and all
Those who are weak and old

Take care of themselves in daily life
Who may be fragile, too trusting!

Too dependent on selfish mankind
For their daily well being

Human mind is so cunning and clever
But not kind or accommodating

Killing innocent animals for selfish nature
To eat their flesh with pride

Cows, sheep, goat, pigs, tiny chicken and fish
Makes no difference, slaughtering mind

Who they kill, who they butcher on land or sea
Even mighty hump whales

Roaming in the vast, open, deep blue seas
Hunted without to extinction

Laying Oceans bare of sea life, using every means
Tuna, Code, dolphin, mermaid all gone!

Polluting the seas, using as vast dumping ground
With glass, plastic and rubbish

Until life no more in the sea, as barren as it could be
On this once fertile, teaming with life seas

Tampering with nature's creation, destroying life
Say no more, Mother Earth

Who is at the end of her tether with no way out!
Good-by my dear friends

We are destined to meet again hopefully in heaven
Wait with patience and trust

Rising from the ashes of our dis-speakable deeds
We may deserve what we get

Do not rule out fury of hell for greedy human kind
As hell is really what humans deserve!

****

The Window Ledge

Sitting on the window-sill,
Looking at the world go by

Adult, children, men, women
Attending their daily chore

Routine work, school and play
Essential ingredients

For keeping human life alive!
Nature's four seasons

Spring, summer, autumn, winter
Creation of Mother Nature

Arrival of long awaited spring
Brings unbounded joy

Mother Nature in wonder bloom
Carpeting the earth

Colourful petals of spring flowers
Falling from blossoming trees

Apples, pears, plums and peaches
Cherries and blue berries

Shedding their rainbow colour blooms
With formation of tiny fruits

Come summer, strawberries galore
Will ripen into sweet berries

Eggs hatches, little chicks flying
Fluttering their tiny wings

Flying aimlessly, here and there
Enjoying summer sunshine

This is time of life for pampering chicks
Parent birds feeding

Soon, it will be an advent of autumn
Chicks maturing into adulthood

Parent birds did their duty, no more around
It is time to learn, to be self-reliant

Look out for sailors on the frothing sea
In tiny boats, hardly seen

When weather is gloomy and foul
You are a beacon of light

Saving their lives with lighthouse bright
All year round giving light

Just sitting on a narrow window seal
Keeping eye on events nearby

Good dead, helping hand, well appreciated
Never goes unnoticed

So be prepared for a well-deserved reward
Heavenly gift on the way

That will be the end of your misery
Lonely life no more!

****

Mighty Tiger

Lion is the undisputed king of jungle
His rule is unchallenged, supreme

As long as there are no tigers in residence
Tigers are the most hunted wild cats

As dead tigers are worth million or two
Just like elephants, worth more

When they are dead rather than alive
That is the irony of Mother Nature

In creating such noble, unique animals
But not for human exploitation

Lion is a noble, well respected animal
Will only kill when in need

To provide his pride, with a meal or two
When accompanied by cubs

Not yet in their prime to help themselves
These mischievous cubs, their future

Tigers are the prime targets for poachers
Who are after their skin and bones!

While tiger skin fetch fortune on black market
Their skin turned into handbags and shoes

The bones are worth their weight in gold
Chinese use them in medical role

Supposed to keep them healthy and fertile
This house-wife tale set in culture

This is death warrant for so many beautiful tigers
But lions and elephants are also not spared

For one reason or another, economic or money making
Cultural stupidly or sheer ignorance

Money is the main motivator for poachers
Human greed knows no bounds

Ready and willing to kill and plunder Mother Nature
Do humans have any shame or conscious!

"All Mighty" give humans some understanding of Nature
Before it is too late to save the planet

Tigers, lions, leopards, not forgetting chevalier cheetahs
These are graceful creation of Mother Nature

Let us use our human ingenuity to safeguard animals
Great and small, tamed and wild

Dogs, cats and horses, men's best friends and companion
Let Mother Nature, make Heaven on Earth

****

Soul Destroying Wars

World has never been free of wars
Since time immemorial

May it will be civil strife or gorilla war
But worse of all is world wars

Since end of devastating world war two
There has been uneasy peace

Two mighty blocks, West and Soviet Union
Armed to teeth with nuclear weapons

That could destroy world several time over
The fear, no win situation won the day

For the first time since end of world war two
There is somewhat unease peace

Let us not be fooled, Vietnam and Korean wars
Were as destructive as World War Two

Victims of wars are civilians, women and children
No one is safe from the brandishing sward

For what, to feed ego of self-important politicians
War has no causes, only excuses

Greed for more land and subjugate neighbours
Then there is natural wealth

Precious gold, diamonds, platinum, oil and iron ore
Not forgetting water, the diminishing resource

Water is the main ingredient, nectar that sustains life
Turns desert into beautiful oasis

Bright spot in never ending sand dunes with sun so hot
Only desert animals, camels could survive

No one is safe from the wreath of soul destroying wars
Losing men makes women widows

That deprives children of fatherly love in family atmosphere
Growing-up orphans, no one to hold their hands!

War heroes are worshipped if they win the war
But condemned losers, as war criminals

Napoleon, Winston Churchill, Roosevelt and Stalin
Were the winners in history books!

Hitler, Mussolini and Japan were the losing grandee
A war to end all contemporaneous wars

An unachievable noble dream that may be fulfilled
With the fear of all out nuclear wars

That may destroy world, bring civilization to abrupt end
Let us live in perpetual hope!

****

World Cup Fever

World Cup football fever is here, to arm-Chair viewers' delight
Give our team a boost, a send-off to remember

In our Caption marvel, Harry Kane, we have goal scorer supreme
Who would emulate Owen, Linaker, Charlton and Shearer!

Not forgetting unique Wayne Rooney, a player of extraordinary talent
Who leads goal scoring chart with goals number fifty three!

No more magnificent midfielders like Gazza, Kegan, Beckham or Brooking
But plenty of youngsters succeed them in time

The cupboard is not bare; we have ever improving Deli Alli and Rahim Sterling
The fever of anxiety, expectation, reward and romance

Our football nursery and Premier league supreme, watched around the world
Will produce another Bobby Moore to lead the world

How we miss world class goal keepers, late Gordon Bank and Peter Shilton
But in emerging Jordan Pickford, we have new world beater

If we win the long overdue world cup, it would be repeat of lucky 1966
Under Caption marvel Bobby Moor, we won the cup

Hero Geoff Hurst whose hat-trick in extra time won the world cup for us
Against mighty Germany, the best team in Europe for a generation!

United Germany and Italy dominated the early world cup competitions
Winning four times each, only Brazil outshining with five wins

Support our talented team, one and all, as they deserve our devotion
Even if we fail this time, it will not be the end of the world

Last word for maligned Russian Federation, the host of 2018 tournament
Their effort, dedication was beyond belief, discipline supreme

No hooligans, no drunken bravo, Russian thugs kept under lock and key
Although we came third, the performance was bright and cheery

Harry Kane, Captain and footballer supreme, winner of **"Golden Boot"**
Envy of other participants and footballing mad nations

Let us hope this is the beginning of new era in our footballing dream
Have patience, we will be crowned World Champion come 2022.

We could day dream to our heart's delight, live in eternal hope and expectation
That is the name of the game that keeps us united and strong!

Have no fear; England team is on the march with purpose and determination
Led by Gareth Southgate, another Sir Alf Ramsey in making.

Success will be hard to come-by, if FA and Premier League let the nation down
Our league is a honeycomb for foreign players and managers

They earn millions but worse they restrict, block the advent of our players
Unlike Germany, France, Italy and Spain

Where home grown players are appreciated, nurtured into world class players
No wonder France is now a leading footballing nation

Winning World Cup twice, not mentioning champion of Europe with pride
With home grown youngsters ruling the roots, showing French pride!

It is time for FA and money grabbing, foreign owning premier league clubs
To save the nation from becoming a poor footballing nation!

****

Child Labour

Child labour is cruelty beyond human endurance
That helps us Westerners to live in comfort

Luxury we enjoy, totally out of reach for the children
Who live in a developing world!

They struggle all days, come rain or sunshine, heat or cold
For few rupees that hardly buys cup of tea in the West

In the so called developed, rich and supposedly democratic world
Who enjoy life of luxury on the sweat of children!

Their bodies under-developed, due to lack of nutritious food and rest
Run around with heavy loads on their tiny heads

Their feet are bare, covered with cuts, no hats and no shoes to wear
Yet carry heavy loads on their under-developed heads

They work in deep mines, cold and damp, dark and dangerous
Digging for diamonds or fool's gold regardless!

Mainly for coal, that heats up our homes and power factories
Creating wealth, comfort and life of luxury

For privileged few, brought-up in lap of luxury, never knew hunger
Ignorant of struggle, life at the bottom end

Children work in fields, in open air, cutting and gathering crops
Picking strawberries and raspberries in season

For us to enjoy with cream, in the comfort of our own homes
Watching Wimbledon tennis in the lap of luxury

World is divided, in East and West, rich and poor, Far and Near
"Have and Have Not" one struggling for a decent meal

While others feast on unhealthy fast food, take away pizza and kebab
Straining their bodies, putting their health at risk

Over eating, obesity that will be the final nail on their body-coffin
Early departure, premature, unexpected death

Due to their life-style, their day to day existence without a care
Carry on regardless, will be the unexpected end.

****

73

Roses

Roses are red, white, cream, yellow, blue and even light green
No matter what colour, every one's favourite flower

The aroma, sweet, pleasant smell, subtle pervasive atmosphere
Fills the summer air with undiluted delight and love

Roses are every one's favourite, no matter what may be the occasion
Birthdays, valentine, engagement or marriage

Roses are ever present to grace the occasion, light the environment
Make everyone happy, cheery and in party mood

One single red rose, unite two lonely hearts, on a valentine day
Union of two souls turn into lifelong engagement

Love shines like a magic cheery tree in full blossom in early spring
Carpeting mother earth with soft, colourful petals

Fashions come and go; yet sweet smelling flowers glow with time
But irreplaceable Red Roses are always there

This sweet smelling bunch of roses with inbuilt nectar and perfume
New colour, new breed never stop developing

Queen Elizabeth, Queen Mother, Princess Diana and many more
Names given in memory of loving, caring dignitaries

Who serve the humanity with care and kindness, without rewards!
So do your best, recognition is always there!

****

Life's Complications

What is life is a million dollar question!
People ask me all the time

What is right, what is good in life today!
May be wrong tomorrow

Failure, success, changes like English weather
Here today, gone tomorrow

Life is like desert mirage, with many interpretations
May be it is unfulfilled dream

Think positive, believe in karma, have trust in God
Then you may never go wrong!

Today it is sunshine, tomorrow laden with grey clouds
Followed by rain, sleet and soft cuddly snow

Life is but a dream, when you wake up, it is reality
Do not waste this God send opportunity

Human life's precious; use it for advantage of mankind
Do not let irritation drag you down

Do not let precious life put you in "No Man's Land"
Neither here nor there, every where

In between cultivated heaven and imaginary hell
No matter what, come Hell or High Water

Devil or deep blue sea, nothing ventured, nothing gained
Remain steadfast, held on to your principle

Life goes on, no matter what, one born every minute
Have faith in "All Mighty

You will certainly have your day in heavenly court!
As sure as night followed by day!

****

English Rose

England, my England is a land of milk and honey
Where countryside is green and pleasant

Four seasons are clearly marked and well defined
Long awaited advent of spring is a delight

Roses are in buds, waiting for the summer sunshine
To blossom, fill the atmosphere with sweet smell

Nature's blossom, however great attraction it may be
There is another English Rose equally great

English girls, young, charming and beautiful lasses
Could fill any one's heart with delight

They are so beautiful, covered with milky complexion
Tall, slim and perfect in development

Curves in all the right places with nature taking care
Carefree, talented and every one's friend

Beauty, charm, friendly nature and heart as good as gold
What more one may want from English Rose!

Your long beautiful hands with long reach and soft touch
Touches my heart, my face and forehead

Expression of affection, dignified in each and every way
Impossible not to fall in love with such a Rose!

Such a Rose is delicate in every way, with soft, kind heart
That falls in love in natural way

So treasurer, cherish such a rose, unique in many ways
Your life long partner, never to be separated

In health and sickness, poverty and wealth
Will be your right hand man

A valuable, priceless asset that will never depreciate
Until call of Nature no one can ignore!

India's Struggle For Independence

India's unique struggle for independence from British Raj
Led by one and only Mahatma Gandhi

His unique, sophisticated, untried nonviolent civil disobedience
Without lifting a finger in anger

That won Mohandas Gandhi, the respect of the entire world
But not the prestigious noble peace prize

Mighty British Empire that ruled supreme over entire India
Over one third of the world as well

From East to West, North to South, with colonies everyway
From Hong Kong to British Guiana

British Colombia, Canada to the remote Falkland Island
Sun never used to set on British Empire

Putting even mighty ancient Roman Empire in purple shade
British might supreme, rule unchallenged

Until one and only Gandhi took up the challenge in earnest
With his modesty, untried and untested

Peaceful challenge to stir British conscious called it satyagrah
So unique, took Britain by surprise

Mighty British Empire did not know for the first time how to fight back
Tried every trick, using brutal force, peaceful talk

In the end every avenue was closed to save the crown jewel
That is India, heart of British Empire

Beginning of World War Two, put hold on Gandhi's move
India understood the evil of Hitler's nationalism

Gandhi cooperated until the end of cruel war in East and West
But did not bring relief to Britain on world stage

Politically drained, economically bankrupt, socially challenged
Britain had no answer to Congress's cunningness

Led by Gandhi, Sardar, Nehru and Bose, not forgetting Dr Ambedkar
Britain who fought Hitler for freedom and equality

Rejecting Hitler's claim, Germans being super race, born to rule the world
Giving Gandhi and Congress superior moral stand

When Winston Churchill, the hero of WW2, saviour of the British nation
Lost 1945 election, Labour forming the government

Under the premiership of aptly named Clement Atlee, with supreme talent
In his Cabinet were best of British brains

Names like Ernest Bevin, Foreign Secretary, Huge Dalton, the Chancellor
James Ede Home Secretary, Herbert Morrison Deputy PM

One and only hero, fiery Welshman Aneurin Bevan, Health Secretary
Who gave us NHS, under Welfare State!

The change of government led to change of priorities, to wind of change
Empire mentality was no longer a priority

Socialist Labour government with landslide election win under their belt
Gave Gandhi and India their well-deserved freedom

On 15th of August 1947, the tricolour Indian flag was raised at midnight
PM Nehru addressing the nation from the Red Fort

Raising fluttering tricolour Indian flag, in every village and town as well
Bringing unbridled joy and happiness in every heart

Playing the Indian national Anthem "Jana Gana Mana" for the first time
Composed by Nobel Literary prize winner Rabindranath Tagore

But India was divided, Muhamad Ali Jinnah outsmarting the entire Indian
Congress
The partition followed by bloodbath with a million dead

India, Pakistan became independent Commonwealth Nations, Delhi India's
Capital
While Pakistan divided into East and West

Neither Gandhi who was assassinated, nor Jinnah who died of natural causes
Lived long enough to see their beloved Motherland

Progressed on path of independence, one secular nation, other staunch Islamic
nation
One economically successful while other on downward slippery slope

This is bitter sweet story of India's struggle for independence from mighty
British Raj
And onward march for success and salvation of the mother nation!

****

Summer Time

Summer time is here, make the most of it
Plenty of day long sunshine

Attractive, warm evenings, gift of Mother Nature!
Long uncomplicated shadows

Gift of the setting sun in the blue cloudless sky
Enhanced one's delight to no end

Reflection in the pond full of water and lilies
Too tempting not to take a dip

To give relief to tiring body, soul and mind!
After all, it is summer time!

Roses are in full bloom, so are sun flowers
Jasmine and Queen of the Night

Spreading sweet, pleasant smell, making my day
Cold drinks are in demand

But for most children, ice-cream is top of the list
Only question is which flavour!

There is vanilla, strawberry, mango and orange
But every one's favourite is chocolate

Decorated with flaky bar and dark chocolate sauce
The choice will never go wrong

Every one's favourite, Children, adults, makes no difference
They all like dark, sweet chocolate

It cools the body, relaxes the mind, lifts the spirit in time
To end the day-outing with setting sun

Children not eager to go home, as it is super holiday time
No early morning wake-up calls to ignore

Dad go to work, mum stays behind to look after the brood
Gives us freedom, to stay in bed to our hearts' delight

As long as we wake up before the end of breakfast time
Oh God! Give us summer time, all year round!

Freedom Misconception

Freedom is such a sweet, sweet word
With different meaning to every one

Economic freedom, political freedom
Then there is social, personal freedom

Freedom of speech, freedom of worship
Freedom from torture, right to feel free

Right to work to support the family's need
If stomach is empty, suffering from hunger

Children go to sleep on empty stomach
Thus freedom is unaffordable luxury!

So called freedom is spoilt rich man's toy
Politicians' conscious in hour of need

Freedom goes hand in hand with responsibility
One without other is morally unacceptable

Unmitigated freedom is like loose cannon
Used by clever, crooked politicians

Like Hitler, Mussolini and Mao to enslave their people
Hypnotised, tortured and subjugate man-kind

Transforming politics into complicated chess game!
For the privileged few born in right families

Economic freedom under capitalism may work wonder
For lucky few, while others may struggle

To put food on table at dinner time for a family of four
Some live in lap of unbelievable luxury

While others shiver, sleeping outdoor in bitterly cold winter
Rich getting richer, without much effort

While poor are thrown on scrap heap without second thought
Sleeping rough, surviving on charity

Goodwill of other passer-by who throw scrap metal coins
To ease their guilty conscious

How could we accept, tolerate such variation in our life-style!
With "Have and Have Not" gap widening all the time

Some are born in Royalty; others gate-crash high society
Count your blessings with roof over your head

If you have three square meals a day, blessed with robust health
For some sleeping around is freedom

Loyal to no one, enjoying graphic satisfaction in one night stand
That is road to ruins in most circumstances

Hunting wild animals, tigers, rhinos, lions, taking pervert delight
In the slaughter of these innocent animals

For their skins, tusks and bones used in ancient Chinese medicine
In the lone hope that it will cure all ills

If this is supposedly freedom, then perhaps totalitarian regime is heaven
Freedom is interpreted in many ways

To exploit fellow human in name of freedom for one's selfish nature!
Could freedom be a myth to trap and rob innocent people!

****

Myriad Rainbow Colours

Rainbow, on a rainy day is an eye-catching display of nature's beauty
Seven interwoven colours going their separate way

Well hidden, invisible from the view during bright, warm and sunny days
Only separated when passing through mist and spray

It needs light rain and sunshine, all at the same time, in cloudless sky
To make the eye catching spectacle to delight man-kind

So monsoon and rainy season is the best time to catch a rainbow glimpse
To make acquaintance of beauty with seven colours!

Colourful rainbow, a nature's precious gift, perfect example of rags to riches
Turns the sky into a desert bloom!

Up above, high in the sky, brightening up horizon with unparalleled beauty
The mist, water vapour splitting Sun's rays

Thus emerging beauty of seven colours hidden in the Sun's bright rays
Unique rainbow is God's gift to brighten our lives

Rainbow is indeed a nature's miracle, a God's gift to living creature
Do not let it go without a glance at nature!

Enjoy, treasure, digest and appreciate God's gift while the spectacle last
If you miss, will have a long wait for re-emergence!

Red, blue, yellow, purple, orange, green, and violet, these are visible colours
Hidden are sage, aqua, coral and indigo colours

The truth is the rainbow contains million colours, for us an unsolved puzzle
Why worry, a puzzle becomes dull fact if resolved

For some rainbow a is beautiful bunch of flowers high in the cloudless sky
Violet, roses, daffodils and tulips, all at the same time

Not forgetting English and African marigolds with sweet smelling jasmines
These are popular flowers gracing English gardens

Parks, roundabouts, open spaces, roadside curbs, not forgetting hanging baskets
That summer-long beautifies English cities

Every one's favourite flowers are red roses that grace each and every occasion
Flowers are for all seasons, for young and old

Engagement, marriage, valentine and birthdays, even for hospital visits
Are not complete without a bunch of flowers

Even funerals are not forgotten, lilies grace these sad occasions
So enjoy the spectacle, immerse in colours

Make the hay while the sun shines, as tomorrow is not certain
We are here today, gone tomorrow

That is way of the world, no matter how high is your standing and honour
We are all equals in the eyes of Mother Nature

****

Women Scorned

Women, on most part are kind, caring and strong
That is why women are rarely scorned

There is no substitute for caring loving mother supreme
Who would go any length to protect her broom!

From cradle to grave, from childhood to adulthood
Mothers are always there, come what may

So why women are mistreated, neglected, cheated by men
Women seeking shelter in Refuge Center

Safety not so much for her, but for her helpless children
Mother would readily sacrifice her life

To protect her children, bring them up in safe environment
Putting mother's love and duty above all

God gave men physical strength, supposed to protect them all
But men are men, not much common-sense!

Their main aim and purpose in life is to enjoy till drop dead
Life is God's gift, enjoy but not waste!

They brutalize, beat-up, scorn, even rape helpless women
Who will one day teach men unforgettable lesson!

Scorned women will spit fire and flame in uncontrolled rage
Will tear men to shred before they come to sense

Like a Spanish matador, she will tackle the bull by the horn
Will drain the life with the tip of a sharp sword

But they carry on regardless, without a sense of purpose
Rock around the clock, wasting precious life

Wise, sensible men, will always treat women fair and square
Avoid offending them, making ever-lasting friends

Women are precious assets, would stand by you in time of need
Their faithfulness never waver, come hell or high water

This is how God shaped women, kind and caring in every way
But also morally strong and determined in self-belief!

To raise her family in time not so good, overcoming every obstacle
So give them respect they so richly deserve!

Women do not "Rock around the Clock" wasting God given precious life
Rise from the ashes to take care of men-kind

Scorned woman is indeed an invitation to Yamraj, God of destruction
Who will do his job; bring life to an abrupt end!

****

Cruel Famine

The word famine is so fearful, so frightening
That it passes shiver in human spine

The world has seen many terrifying famines
That has killed so many innocent souls

While Mother Nature may be responsible
For famine, when rainfall denied

Turning Mother Earth into parched, dried earth
Destroying crops, children going hungry

Most famines are caused by selfish human behaviour
Wars, boycott, sanctions and civil unrest

Holding back food supply for political cause
Are the true reasons for hunger!

Some get prosperous, from rags to riches in no time
Hording food from the poor

Until the price is right to swell one's bank balance
Make a killing for a fist full of dollar

The famous famine of Bengal, under British Raj
Millions died while surplus food denied

Punishing innocents, mainly children and old
To fed one's ego at any cost!

Famine shows no sign of retreating, abating soon
Children would not know if or when

The curse of famine, hunger, swollen stomachs
Arms, legs so thin, like weathered sticks

Giving-up hope, no angel of mercy on the horizon
Mum and dad abstain from food

To feed the children from whatever available food
So often on grass, roots and little else

Famine is still unashamedly hovering on the horizon
Many lives lost, family devastated

God decide who to save, who can go, open the door
Of heaven as well as unsavoury hell

The cards of faith have already selected, dispatched
Lucky few were being dealt with aces!

Lottery winners who will live to see the day-light
Not in company of friends and families

Pray All Mighty, no more famine in our life-time
Enough have perished in Yemen famine.

****

Mona Lisa

Beauty of Mona Lisa is beyond question
Beyond human understanding

God created Mona Lisa in his leisure time
To make her perfect, a timeless beauty

Putting her on canvas, making her immortal
That honour goes to master painter

Leonardo Da Vinci who used Lisa Gherardini
As his life model creating Mona Lisa

The mysterious smile that puzzles many critics
Is it a pain or optical illusion!

More demur expression for public to judge
If viewed from different angle

Gives different; confusing interpretation
Creating a puzzle for us to solve

The painting, valued at a hefty billion dollar
No one could afford except

A few oligarch billionaires with billions
Looted from rich and poor

As well as their motherlands with blessings
From the corrupt politicians

The painting rightly belongs to a museum
Where everyone, rich and poor

Can have the pleasure to view in comfort
One and only unique Mona Lisa!

****

Black Madonna of Monserrat

Monserrat, a holy, beautiful hill-station
Is another religious place

In the mould of famous Lourdes in France
High in Pyrenees Mountains

Where pilgrims flock to seek salvation of soul
Drink holly water for miracle cure!

Blessed Montserrat Abby is similarly situated
In Catalonia, near Barcelona

High on Montserrat Multi-peak Mountain
Santa Maria de Montserrat Abby

A treasure of Spain's Catalonia region
Attracting mass pilgrimage

A popular hill station with added bonus
Curing sick with healing power

One and only Black Madonna of Monserrat!
Her spirituality unsurpassed!

Where pilgrims queue up in droves
To hold the hand of Madonna

A favourite place of newly married couples
Where they spend their honeymoon!

Monastery has a long, troubled history
Complicated and bloody

Napoleon sent his army, time and again
To loot, burn and subjugate

Irrepressible Black Madonna of Monserrat
The Abby is a place of learning

Has world famous Chorus of young boys
Cream of Western world!

Young, talented, privileged and pampered
Given the ultimate privilege

To blossom under watchful eye of Madonna
To serve humanity at large!

These children, cream of noble aristocrats
Armed with noble principle

Go out as articulate adults in their prime
Make their name on many fronts!

Serve their motherland with distinction and pride
On political, science and cultural front

Discovering new medicine, painting Mona Liza
Long live Black Madonna of Monserrat.

****

We undertook this journey, this pilgrimage way back in 2003, as my editor, Shri Krishan Raleigh wanted me to visit this holy place and write an article. Although suffering from poor health, we did undertake this journey that involves a lot of walking, as well as climbing steep steps. It was a minor miracle that I had no adverse effect, even though we were dead tired at the end of the excursion. Perhaps holding the holy hand of mighty Madonna was a blessing! My article, with beautiful photographs was published in India Link and became an instant hit with readers.

Solitude

Solitude is a sharp, two edge sword
For some it is a God sent gift

While for others, solitude is deathly silence
When they yearn for human company

Humans are social animals, at their best
When surrounded by friends

Humans are not accustomed to solitude
That led them to depression

They react well when in the company
Of their fellow human-beings

So are many wild animals that survive best
When in the company

Of their fellow animals, like lions, elephants
Deer, zebras and gorillas

Living in groups, help them survive
Raise their young ones

Hunting in harmony, to catch their preys
That feeds the Lion Pride

Baby elephants are so cute, cuddly and affectionate
But helpless without the protection

Of their mothers' milk and the elephant herd
Led by a strong bull, father figure

My solitude is unique, not in public domain
I gaze and stare at moon lit night

Building sand castles that may not survive
In the warmth of emerging day light!

When the world sleeps in solitude silence
Dropping soft cotton-wool snow

In abundance, from the moon lit night sky
Dawn not that far behind

I stare at the golden nugget in heavenly sky
This will melt like an iceberg!

When it drifts away from its natural home
To the beauty of tropical warmth

In the heat of the bright, hot mid-day sun
That inevitably follows early dawn

Time will come in haste, scattering sunlight
Brighten the day for people in flight!

On their way to work, earn their daily bread!
To feed the family of two plus two

This is their daily routine, everyone has to follow
With silver solitude and expectant hearts

****

Mother's Love

Mother's unselfish love is a God sent gift to humanity
Caring for her children, come hell or high water

Thinking about my mother, kind, caring and supreme!
Taking care of us, all round the year

When I was young, innocent but never the less mischievous
She was always there, fixing my broken bones

My mother is my heart, my soul, my dignity, my tool to succeed
Turn my dreams, my ambition into reality

When drowning in a shallow, a foot of muddy rain water
She is always there to teach me how to swim

How to navigate the life full of unexpected obstacles
Come out strong and mentally alert

She is always there to comfort me, in my time of sorrow
When my ego is battered and bruised

To whom I turn for moral support in time of adversity
One and only my true love beyond question

She is wise, full of ancient wisdom, could solve every puzzle
With ease and knowledge stored in her heart and mind!

Mother's love is supreme, for her every child, boy or girl is special
Gender makes no difference, no preference

Planning my future, my destiny, seeking partner so early in life
Girlfriend problems, seeking mother's advice!

After all, she has experienced all these situations in her life
Many worse situations that made her wise!

With my best interest at heart, I listen to her advice without doubt
Now a young man, stepping out alone

Residing with fellow students in the university's resident compound
Missing my mum's cooking, my evening meal

That kept me well fed, healthy, strong body and worldly wise
Beyond my years that brings wisdom wise!

Modern invention, information technology, kept me in regular touch
That made the separation somewhat bearable!

Come what may, hell or high water, devil or the deep blue sea
My mother is always there, waiting for me!

In her presence, under her guidance, the desert orchid bloomed
Creating an oasis of eternal peace

So drop your ego, touch her feet and pray with her at the altar
Give her a podium seat in your heart

She is the only one who will take you from rags to untold riches
From Pauper to Prince, Sudama to Lord Krishna

Taken for granted, you will only miss her when she is no more
So make most of her company while the sun shines!

****

Power of Poetry

Poetry is a combination of rhymes and rhythms
It is an ancient, precious, progressive art

Glorified in religions, as most holy books are written
In verses, by learned saints and sages

Most visible in the ancient, culturally rich religions
Mighty Mahabharata is a poem written

In ten thousand verses, in ancient language Sanskrit
The basis of all modern languages

So is Ramayana, the story of Lord Rama and Lady Sita
That captivates the literary world

Name of supreme writer Shakespeare, dominates stage
With plays like Julius Caesar

Not forgetting Hamlet, Othello, Macbeth, Romeo and Juliet
A tip of iceberg, making him national poet

These plays are performed every day by actors' best
In front of appreciative audience

In the throbbing heart of literary London that excels
When it comes to culture, art and science

Popular English language is blessed with so many literary giants
That includes talented Bronte sisters

Then there are modern talented attics, likes of Agatha Christie
Who churns out novels like a conveyer belt!

Most popular, at least amongst children is J. K. Rowling
Who gave us one and only Harry Potter

Her books turned into memorable Hollywood films
Made her richly deserved millions

Children are spell-bound, mesmerized, reading her every book
So do adults, sharing children's inquisitive mind!

My favourite author is clever and cunning Sir Arthur Conon Doyle
Whose works include creation of Sherlock Holms!

A crime fighter, detective supreme, who would solve every crime
With ease, using his super mind!

His creation "Hounds of Baskerville" performed universally
To the delight of world-wide audience

Even though I have seen the play performed umpteen times
Yet I throng the theatre whenever nearby

I enjoy the supreme power of literature, poems, novels and plays
As long as I could, till my dying days?

****

Mystic Universe

Twinkle twinkle my bright little star
High in the clear nighty sky!

So far, yet deceptively so near
But never within our reach

A bright star, shining like a tiny Moon
On a dark, deserted night

Staring down from the Northern sky
With a smile so sweet!

His timely message, so purposeful
Enjoy unique Mother Earth

Blessed with wonderful flora and fauna
Unique in the universe!

Makes human life, wonderful existence!
Being children of Mother Earth

Mother Earth, so fertile, so blessed
With streams, rivers and oceans

Forests, woods and mountain range
Towering mighty Himalayas

The combination makes wonderful Earth
A heaven to habitat for human race!

Himalayas kissing sky like newlywed bride!
Shy but so tempestuous

Enjoying the life that is in full bloom
Make the hay while Sun shines!

Mother Earth, heaven of habitat for human race
One and only inhabited place

In the vast, ever expanding Universe so bright
With no end in sight!

Our Sun, one big ever bright burning star
Sustaining life on Mother Earth

With its warmth and ever bright Sun light
That sustains agricultural paradise!

Where meadows and ever flowing brooks
In the land of the midnight Sun!

Yet we treat Mother Nature with scant respect
Polluting rivers, seas and oceans

Killing fish, dolphins, sharks and mighty whales!
With polluting plastic waste

A by-product and excesses of greedy human race
Who will destroy one and only

Green, Green, Mother Earth, bringing human race
To an abrupt end!

Wake up you greedy humans before it is too late
That will spell the end of human race!

****

Beauty of African Wilderness

Wilderness is a God's wonderland
Blessed with rugged beauty

Where wild animals roam in freedom
Ideal home for God's creation

Wilderness abounds in wild Africa
Known as Dark Continent

A huge, mighty continent of contras
Everyone wants to explore

Landmass of ever-changing beauty
Topography to savour!

Mighty Sahara desert dominates
The heart-land of Africa

Chain of snow-capped Atlas Mountains
Dominates Northern African sky

Beautifying surrounding countries
Morocco main beneficiary!

With vast lakes and mighty rivers galore
The Nile, world's longest river

The cradle of early mighty civilization
That stamped its mark

On the surrounding nations like Egypt
The land of mighty pyramids

Temples of Luxor Khonsu and Kom Ombo
On the bank of river Nile

These temples so ancient, yet so beautiful
Heart of a tourist nation!

Lake Victoria, vast inland overflowing sea
That is the source of river Nile

Snow-capped rugged Mount Kilimanjaro
Gentle yet challenging

A dream adventure for every mountaineer
A heaven for African wild life

Where vast herds of elephants roam freely
Along with lions and rhinos

Land of thousand wonders, beauty and beast
A dream reserve for animal life

Vast Serengeti Plain and Lake Manayara
The only place on Earth

Where lions climb trees, dragging their preys
To keep their kill safe

From sky full of opportunist vultures that devour
Any flesh, fresh or rotten!

Keeping forest clean, healthy habitable place
For humans, Masai tribe!

So when you plan your next annual holiday
Keep Africa in mind

Especially Kenya, Tanzania, Uganda and above all
South Africa, most popular destination

My favourite, beautiful, wild Ngorongoro Creator
One of seventh natural wonder

That will keep you mesmerized, under spell
Of unparalleled African beauty

My homeland, my dreamland Dar es Salaam
On the shores of Indian Ocean

Where we spend our childhood, our best days
Remembered with haunting memory

How we miss this vast, open land of Tanzania
And the beautiful people

Kind caring and peaceful, unlike rest of Africa
Long live Tanzania, heaven on Earth!

****

Warrior Tribe Masai

Masai Mara, unique game reserve without parallel
In the heart of wild Africa

Sharing this beautiful landscape with Masai tribe!
A proud and elegant ancient pride

That lives, survives and flourishes in traditional style
Tried and tested lifestyle

Suited for nomadic life, cattle their pride and wealth
Cattle, kind of ancient currency

Given as valued gift when socially seeking bride!
Enhancing social standing in the tribe!

Depending on the quality and size of the cattle herd
One may own and treasure

That stops unnecessary slaughter that is the hallmark
Of wasteful Western life-style!

Masai, well known for their courage and unique lifestyle
Feared and loved in equal measure

In reality, Masai are gentle, caring, loyal and kindly tribe
With warm-heart hospitality

For one and all, who come to realise their unique culture
By spending their time with Masai tribe!

Masai is a warier tribe with staple diet of milk and blood
That keeps them strong and healthy!

When Masai youth in his prime, ready to enter adulthood
Has to kill a lion with his shield and spear

He is then accepted as an adult, ready to settle in married life
His parents start seeking bride

Paying bride-price with herd of cattle that enables the couple
To settle down and start family life

Masai tribe is close-net family, with moto share and share alike
No one neglected, everyone looked after

Young, old, healthy, sick, wealthy and poor makes no difference
Prince and pauper equally respected

Masai lives in kibbutz style, village on the move entire life
One for all and all for one

The old, brave, tried and tested Masai solder never dies
Only fades away with time

That is how this nomadic, ancient, venerable tribe survives
This is Africa, God's blessed continent.

****

Gypsy

The word Gypsy creates different feelings
In different minds

For some Gypsies are wonderful people
God's own creation!

Roaming freely in nomadic life of their own choice
Enjoying nature at its best

Here today, gone tomorrow, no fixed abode
That is the beauty

Of their wondering, nomadic, carefree life
One may envy or dislike

Their lifestyle, their existence, their aim in life
But they love it, treasure it

That matters most, creating unique, happy lifestyle
Give them some respect

Some breathing space, to live unhindered life
After all, Gypsies' are God's children

Who deserves some respect, longevity of life!
Like us, normal people

Who monopolies and dictate every-day life
Expecting others to follow

Every arrow we throw with blind expectation
It rarely hits the expected target

Without a question, doubt or a shred of evidence
That ours is superior lifestyle!

Our minds are like an uncaged monkey
Rushing from here to there

In search of purpose and happy life-style!
That eludes us most of the time

Seek the help of "Happy Pills" on GP prescription
That makes life drug dependent

So let us open our mind, learn different lifestyle
That may surprise us

Make friends, harvest hey while sun shines bright
Create first class environment

That make us tolerant of different culture, different values
Live together in perfect harmony

One for all and all for one, is Gypsy's moto, way of life
Stand side by side in adversity

Gypsy unites; support each other in their hour of need
Friendship and unity is their way of life

Building togetherness Baily Bridges, crosses obstacles
To make Earth, a heaven on earth!

****

Land of Rising Sun

Industrious Japan, known throughout
The world, far and near

As the prosperous Land of Rising Sun
With charming beautiful people

Not blessed with natural resources
Rugged and over-crowded

But people are happy and contended
Life's longevity unsurpassed

Prone to natural disasters earth-quake!
A frequent uninvited visitor

Japan lying on the rim of fault-line
Delicately balanced

The fault line stretches from California
To Alaska and beyond

Affecting Indonesia and Philippines
Not forgetting Japan

A prosperous nation of Rising Sun
With high living-standard

An envy of entire civilized world!
Striving to catch up Japan

That rest of us can only dream about!
In envy and admiration

In equal terms and equal measures
To follow this mighty nation

Japan's wealth is its human population
So devoted, so honest

Articulate, highly educated, hard working
With their superior culture

Japan is the work horse of the entire world
Their inventions much appreciated

Their products, cars, TVs and electronics
Always in great demand

Their religion Shintoism, kind of Buddhism
That keeps the society safe

From the ills and advances of the tired West
That keeps us in perpetual mess

Morally declined and culturally drained West
Where no one is really safe

From knife violence that is gripping the nation
Parents grieving at the loss

Of their young, beautiful and talented children
Victims of mindless thuggery

No one knows how to abate tide of self-harm
Or give the police helping hand!

So let Japanese culture be our guardian angel
To lead us to promised land

A beautiful, green, green land of milk and honey
To savour our remaining days!

The land we call England, ancient, well respected
Take pride, call yourself Englishman!

****

Rags to Riches

Life is but an unpredictable dream
Full of promises when asleep!

Dreams melt away without a trace
In the reality of early dawn!

Dreams are dreams, may come and go
Appear and disappear

But life is a reality, it must go on
Come hell or high water

Life is not a midnight mystery
Nor is a bed of roses

It will take you from rags to riches
With All Mighty blessings

All it needs is a positive mental attitude
Bit of faith will not go unnoticed!

Glass may be half full but never half empty
With positive mind and attitude

We need faith, from cradle to grave
To rise from ashes!

This is land of honey and opportunities
So do not give up hope!

Life's midnight mystery will resolve itself
In the reality of sunny day

Come with me on the journey of discovery
To find your promised land

If there is wish, then there is certainly a way
To resolve your problems

For once and all, never to come back to haunt
With the blessings of Mighty God!

So reflex, take deep breath, enjoy the fresh air
Your good days are on the horizon!

****

Storm In A Tea Cup

Life is what you make of it
Could be heaven on earth

It could be a hell in the making
You are in charge to shape it

As you wish, as you may desire
But do not let it be a chance!

Make it lottery due to lack of efforts
On your part, you may regret

Do not let a storm in a tea-cup
Derail your sweet dreams

Your rags to riches ambition
Will take time and effort

To turn it into a lifelong reality
Never be fooled

Never imagine life a bed of roses
Even roses have thorns

One may have to lie on bed of nails
That is called ups and downs

Of our every day, ever changing life-style
Make most of it while sun shines

Glass may be half full or half empty
It is your interpretation

That will decide the glass capacity
Be positive, have faith

Trust your instinct, never be in despair
Positive thinking wins battles

109

They knew not what they want in life
Do not let sell by date

To overtake your shelve-life in ignorance
Like a flower that has withered

Without ever blossoming, in full bloom
A waste of wonderful life

There would be no joy, no satisfaction
If every day was the same

Like bright sunshine in tropical climate
Where people long for cloudy sky!

Rain in desert welcoming, life-sustaining sight
That turns Mother Earth green

Desert blooms, covered with thorny flowers
Bloom for a short while

Before nature takes charge, back to routine
Dust to dust, ashes to ashes

Dreams not last long, disappear with day-light
Right attitude, positive thinking

Makes a difference the way we live our lives
Even if for a short while

Be positive, have right attitude, never despair
Forget storm in tea cup

Hope for the best while the Sun shines bright!
Take nothing for granted in life!

****

Our Care-Free Lives

Our care-free life in East Africa
A heaven on Earth

I was born, brought-up in Tanzania
In city of Dar Es salaam

A popular, imaginative Arabic word
Means Gateway to Heavens!

City on the shores of Indian Ocean
With heavenly weather

Not so cold or hot, tolerable weather
May be some times

Too hot to handle in mid-December
But cool breeze from mighty

Indian Ocean, that keeps it cool
And tolerable weather

Outdoor life, a gift from heaven!
Most suited for barbeque

In the cool of the setting Sun
On sandy beach heaven

Watching boats sailing by
Over Ocean waves

Drinking nectar coconut water
As sweet as heavenly water

Playing music, Indian film songs
On outdated gramophone

That is an unmissable occasion
Not much appreciated

Or missed by local people, as it is
An everyday occurrence!

That is norm throughout the world
What is on our door-step!

Taken for granted, God's given gift
Until it is no more!

Gone with the wind, blown away for good
That is unenviable nature

So make the hay while the Sun shines
Before the advent of cloudy sky

Reserve your place in heavenly Dar
Make it your last resting place!

****

Migration

There is always one reason or another
To move, to uproot one's family

Desert one's natural birth-place, habitat,
Without a second thought

Even if it could be a heaven on Earth
For every residing human

Where we could swim in cool water!
At day break with rising Sun

To cool and refresh the aching body
Before advent of day's work!

Call from foreign land of pasture green
Too tempting to ignore

May sound like a heaven on Earth!
From a distance long

Like a mountain, high and majestic
Until you see it from near

Huge, lacklustre boulders of clay
Of no importance to nature

With thinly covered coarse grass
Not fit for grazing animals

Waste of valuable space that is nature
The teasing Mother Earth

Could not be a heaven for humans
Who least deserves

A Garden of Eden for their pleasure!
Reserved for special persons!

We go back to Dar but not that often
As our busy lives here

Are not beds of roses, as envisaged!
When we left Dar in hurry

But bygone is bygone, mistake made
Don't cry over spilled milk

Life may be tough in Promised Land
But future is bright

For the children in green, green land
Blessed with culture

Education is more important in life
Than temporary pleasure

So do not be sad or down-hearted
Move has worked wonder!

A hidden meaning, God's intention
For welfare of the family!

All's well that ends well is prime moto
The move has been a great success!

Rejoice, have picnic on summer's evening
On a long, hot and bright day

When the Sun do not set until mid-night
On this beautiful blessed land!

That is England, land of milk and honey
Where roses bloom

There are two types of English roses
One that adorns gardens

Other that turns home into heaven
A delicate beauty

She is much in demand every where
But only a lucky few

May get the opportunity to tie the knot
Bring her home

A home that is Englishman's castle
To protect and cherish

An English rose in full bloom
Beauty never in doubt

A life partner, never to be separated
Live happily ever-after!

****

Love Me Tender

Love me tender, love me often
Love me all the time

Love me night or day, at any time
That makes my day!

Love is the name of the sulky game
We play all the time

Love always triumphs, conquers all
Without a shot being fired

In anger or worry or in anxiety
That is a common cord

Life is but a short, sharp dream
Disappears with light of day

Dreams may put you in wonder land
But it does not last that long

Reality is the name of this game
That soon takes life over

When I was young, I had a dream
To make world go round

One for all and all for one every time
No matter how many times

In stark reality, life is in a nut-shell
Here today, gone tomorrow

So make hay while the Sun shines
Life is too short to waste

Have positive attitude, trust in God
He will always be there

Every time, come Hell or High Water
That is name of the game

We play all the time, with friends or foes
In sickness and health

It is an addiction beyond our control
Be aware before you are trapped!

Once caught in iron jaw, its' difficult to get out
However hard you may try

It is the law of mighty nature for one and all
So don't feel you are alone

Passage of time may dull the pain in due course
But scars will always remain

They are constant reminder of past misdeeds
To make sure you go straight

If you learn from your many past mistakes
Wounds' worth its weight in gold!

My trust in mighty Lord Krishna is unshakeable
That has stood the test of time

Make my complicated life, not a bed of roses
But gives me comfortable life-style!

That I deserve, having worked hard all the time
The reward for work ethic supreme!

****

Is Life a Puzzle!

Life is neither heaven nor hell
It is what you make of it

It could be heaven on Mother Earth
If you play your cards right

It could be unimaginable hell
If you fail to appreciate!

God has created Mother Earth
So green, fertile, beautiful

Colourful, sweet smelling flowers
Not forgetting tasty fruits

Bananas, Pomegranates, Pineapples
Mangos, Guavas, Oranges

All are tropical fruits, full of juice
Products of sunshine plenty

Then there are Apples, Grapes and Olives
Products of Mediterranean climate

Yielding wine, whisky and olive oil
Main dishes of Western food

Don't surrender to Abrahamic morality
Misled by fool's gold!

That sustains our life as we know it
Humans are not sole residents

On this beautiful planet Mother Earth
Covered with Tropical Forests

Tundra, Sahara desert and Artic Circle
Land topography as diverse

And fertile as human imagination
That knows no bounds!

Colonies of colourful Birds of Paradise
Peacocks, Parrots and Partridges

Then there are common birds like pigeons
Crows, Cuckoos and eagles

Then there are animals, wild and tamed
Small, large, on land and ocean

Hostile, gentle and tamed, friends and foes!
Natural allies of humans

That keeps our lives going with milk and honey
Cattle, pigs, sheep and chicken

Farmed with extreme cruelty, bled to death
To satisfy our buds of taste

A cruel, shameful side of greedy humanity
Who would go to any length!

To establish human superiority over all
Creatures, great and small

Gathering of every one under one roof
Meant to live in peace, harmony

Its' time for humans to be wise and caring
Not after the events

Would be too late, destroy human existence
Gone like mighty dinosaurs

Dead as dodo, hunted to extinction for pleasure
A deep wound on Mother Earth!

****

Human Greed

Human Greed knows no bounds
That is their downfall

Humans destroy natural habitat
Making wild-life homeless

That makes no sense to human mind
Why stab ourselves in the back!

Humans infected with satanic pride
Part of unanimity

We share dreams, expectations
No matter what's our aim!

Jumping from one tree to another
Like an uncaged monkey

Humans, foot lose and fancy free
Lost in maze

Looking for purpose in their life
That happens to be nearby!

Humans play games with Nature
Know not what they want!

Keep on destroying, burning forests
In vain hope of finding gold!

Gold and diamonds, already mined
From deep underground mines

Being catalyst of our own dreams
Of satanic pride

God made thee humans supreme
To be our guardian angel!

Let us be protector of Mother Nature
To justify the faith

That responsibility God imposed on us
Let's not let-down Mother Earth!

God made us, humans supreme
To be protector of Nature!

That is how real lives evolves in time
So make the most of nature

Let humans be protector of the weak
Prove their worth with actions

Time is short, here today, gone tomorrow
That is name of the game

So make most of God send opportunity
Before time runs out!

Make your pedigree reflect your blue blood
Don't preach on empty belly

Once innocence is lost, virginity no more
Something no one can restore

Not even God, however hard he may try
So act with care and consideration

For human life is a valuable gift from God
Treasure, cherish it for ever!

****

Laughter Is The Best Medicine!

An apple a day, keeps doctor away
Laughter an hour

Keeps depression, loneliness at bay!
Without an input

Of drugs from medical profession
The easy remedy

Seeking answer for our troubles
Pills for every ill

From cradle to grave, till the end
Carry on regardless

How nice if laughter could be
Provided on NHS

Live a life of unbridled exhilaration
Cultivate inner harmony

As we are all victims of living
In ever-changing world!

But not for the better or gentler
Benefiting humanity

We love to live in modern world
Brainwashed by media

To be happy, rich and famous
Act in Indian movies!

A tale of two cities far apart
In complicated term

Cultivate DNA of self-enlightenment
With unbridled exhilaration

From rags to riches are our wishes
A desert in bloom

Migration from villages to cities
Overflowing humanity!

Come with great expectations
Like cotton-wool kids
Make millions without shedding tears
As easy as watching

Addicted to endless Indian movies
Cheap entertainment

Where the hero always gets the girl
Of his dream

No matter what the social, cultural divide
May be or not

Get married, live happily ever-after
That is film ending

****

Cheap Escapism

An escaping from torturing reality
Even if for a moment

Its' better for soul and tiring body
Simmering with rage

The false anxiety, full of suspicion
Mind over matter

That rules entire life of confusion
Even if without truth

Failure to realize one's sweet dream
Leads to anger

The word "Anger" is only one letter
Short of word DANGER!

So do not retreat to bunker of despair!
Aim your laser beam

Where it will do more good than harm
Fulfilling wonderful mantra!

Rags to riches is not one day wonder
Will take time and sacrifice

Each and every day to achieve success
Until the desert blooms!

Our determination, resolves are tested
In time of adversity

We are mere puppets controlled by
Twin short strings

Joy and sorrow, health and happiness
Charted by "All Mighty"

When we are born with such a delight
Hearts overflowing

With flutter, joy and expectations high
For every family member

Don't leave quality of life to chance
Fight for the right

Make it your choice, look for your partner
Not someone you could live with

But someone you could not live without
Now and never

****

Setback In Life

May have numerous setbacks in life
Make it personal odyssey

The real conviction, steadfast self-belief
Of any importance

Shed righteous, overbearing self-certainty
In favour of modesty

Install the DNA of self-enlightenment
Unbridled exhilaration

So make hay while the sun shines
Rays of midday sun

Noon warmth and sun will not stay
Lingering on for long

In clear blue sky of hope, expectation
Under bright shining Sun

So much loved, want more sunshine
Life sustaining Sun

Before advent of inevitable evening
Domain of setting Sun!

On distant horizon of faraway sky
At the end of the day

Setting sun disappearing beyond horizon
Followed by night

Inevitably dark, moonless, nocturnal night
Until dawn takes over!

When circle of hope and disappointment
Going round time and again!

Believe or not, that's life, for one and all
No matter what!!

So often a blind leads another blind
Put it in nut shell

Be street wise, grab the opportunity
Live happily ever after!

For human life is one-off gift from God
Enjoy it in full

Don't forget your fellow human beings
Most are kind, caring

Take short cut favoured by All Mighty
To the gates of Heaven!

Where Virgin Mary and Lord Jesus Christ
Ready to embrace thy presence!

****

What A Wonderful World!

What a wonderful world we live in
A God's gift to man-kind!

As different as chalk and cheese
Vast empty Sahara desert

Home to on the move nomadic tribes
Camels, their priceless possessions

Life sustaining all round partners
In time good and bad

Desert, vast and full of sand dunes
Shifting, always on the move

Occasionally blessed with oasis
A Garden of Eden

Nature's gift to needy desert dwellers
Place to rest and recuperate

Then there is frozen Artic, Antarctic
Known to one and all

No one wants to visit these wonder lands
Making it a heaven

For unique wild-life, Emperor Penguins
Seals, whales and birds

A safe retreat, far from prying human eyes
That keeps wild-life safe

Bonus for destructive, undeserving human kind
For tomorrow's generation

Growing up children, adults of the future
A preserved paradise!

Five Continents, three mighty roaring oceans
Sustaining every life

Evolved over timeless billion years back
From a tiny cell

To mighty, ever inquisitive human beings
The persistence mankind

Europe, heart of human excellence
Personifies modern life

Home of ancient democracy
The Roman Empire

Magnet of attraction for one and all
Cherishing wealth, prosperity

Sweet honey bee-hive, mighty attraction
Refugees, economic migrants

Who risks their lives, to penetrate Europe!
A mystic, forbidden land

Where streets are paved with imaginary gold
Dreams become reality in no time at all!

****

What A Wonderful World [Continents]
Part Two

Then there is Asia, a mighty continent
Harbouring oldest civilization

Where mighty Himalayas kiss the sky!
Birth place of noble religions

Hinduism, Buddhism, Sikhism, Jainism
Christianity and Islam

Not forgetting Judaism, Zoroastrianism
Pride of ancient Persia

India, China, Russia and industrious Japan
Mighty nations of Asia

Then there is Africa, a virgin continent
A Garden of Eden

Where wildlife roam as freely as could be
Animals, large and small

Lions, Elephants, Rhinos and Hippos
A gift from God

Continent rich in minerals, diamonds and gold
Tanzanite, copper galore!

The continent looted, brutalized and colonized
In the name of progress

Now left to its' fate, struggling to survive
Its' harsh economic reality

Slowly but surely Africa is re-emerging
Taking its reserved place

On the world map, with pride and purpose
As tourism thrives

Tourists, chasing that illusive pot of gold
Unsurpassed beauty

Acquiring inner sense of unique harmony
Unbridled exhilaration

Banishing the den of inherited inequality
Sense of inner pride

Africa, my golden, harmonious Africa
Place of my birth

The beautiful city of Dar standing tall
Facing the mighty Indian Ocean

Thy attractions, beauty, have not dimed
With passage of time

But like maturing wine, has come to age
Giving unique taste

Would like to spend my remaining days
Reminiscing the past

Watching Sun setting, behind ocean waves
Make you feel jubilant!

Until time of departure, path charted by All Mighty
Reunion with Mother Nature!

****

About Author

He was born and brought-up in Dar Es Salaam, Tanzania when it was a British Colony. He describes his early life as tranquil, peaceful and laid-back, as the country was indeed a heaven on earth, a beautiful country beyond imagination, with the romantic Indian Ocean on the door-step where he used to take a dip early in the morning before starting work!

As there was no television and even radio was a luxury in those distant, post-war days, a few can afford, people used to spend most of their free time on the beach, as Dar has one of the most beautiful beaches in East Africa.

This periodic atmosphere is vividly captured in his short story "Heaven on Earth" published in his novel "Ivory Tower" a collection of short stories.

Bhupendra came to London in 1968, just after Tanzania gained independence, where he still resides. He is an accountant by profession but loved writing since his childhood. In 1999 he had a mishap in hospital that changed his life, retired from his accountancy profession and took up writing full-time.

To his great surprise, he found himself good at writing. He started with writing letters to local as well as national newspapers, then moved on to writing articles, newspaper columns, short stories, poems, covering visits of Indian politicians like Narendra Modi, L. K. Advani and interviewing British politicians, MPs, Lords, Mayors and leading personalities from the Asian community.

However he considers his greatest achievement is to write novels and his two popular novels are Ivory Tower and Olive Grove. This book of poems is his first foray into the art of writing poems, the most difficult part of literary writing one could undertake. I hope readers will enjoy and appreciate **"Cry For Help"** as much as his novels.

****

Penny Authors Anthology

Bhupendra's poems have also been featured in the Penny Authors' Anthology, volume 5, titled "Book of Lived".

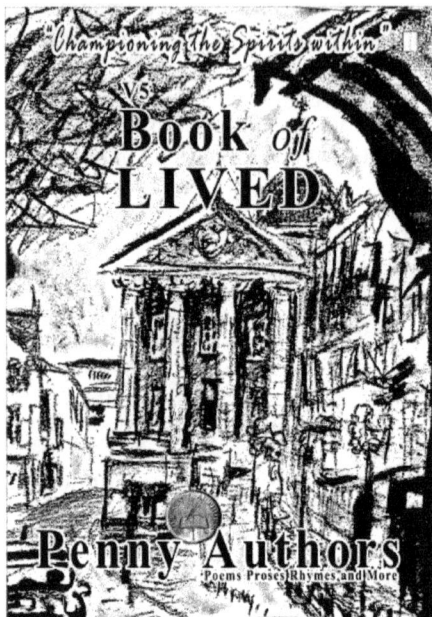

Penny Authors are poets who have come together from all walks of life, from all ethnicity and geographical to social background. Penny Authors is a reach out to all whose who aspire to express their celestial inheritances, the lived life. Share this experience so that others can find their "missing jigsaw piece in their lives".

He has joined an ever growing family and supports the aspiration of all to rise and achieve, and etch in the halls of human existence on this flesh dependent planet.

His and all Penny Authors work touch the central sense of those who read them, only humans will feel the energies within that seeks to insulate the human in all of us. This book is available in all book store and on-line.

What you get with Penny Authors?

- It's free to publish your work
- You become part of the growing family
- You have option to join the voluntary royalty sharing facility
- You benefit from the profit from your book sale
- You benefit from the cooperative promotion and publicity of PA.
- You have the opportunity to continue to publish your work in all future volumes
- You also have the opportunity to publish your own book, this is facilitated through the Penny Authors set up.

For more information about the Penny Authors and how it become part of this special group, email: pennyauthors@yahoo.co.uk.

Index

If you enjoyed this collection then why not check out the others.

****

MA Publisher Catalogue

ISBN/Titles /Image/Author	Descriptions
978-1-910499-02-3 (eBook) & 978-1-910499-00-9 (Paperback) Father to child By Mayar Akash	This EBook version Father to Child is a collection of inspirational poems and musings that follow the author's life from his own childhood up to when he had children of his own, and wishes to pass some of wisdom to them.
978-1-910499-16-0 River of Life By Mayar Akash	This journey in the river of life, a metaphor for living, a contrast between the British life and the Bangladeshi lives' in both parts of the world. Reflect on the integrational change acquired and adopted as a result of living in UK.
978-1-910499-14-6 The Halloweeen Poem By Zainab Khan	This short poetry book written by Zainab who was an 8-year-old. She writes about her experience of Halloween in poetry form, especially as a young Bangladeshi Muslim growing up and integrating into the British society and how these customs have become her school and daily life.

ISBN/Titles /Image/Author	Descriptions
978-1-910499-36-8 Delirious By Liam Newton	Music is powerful enough to change people's views on aspects of the society they live in or the world around them. It magnifies the actual feelings the artist feels and shares with others their experience. In this book the writer gives the reader snapshot insight of his life in the form of lyrics. Music keeps him going and hope it keeps you going too
978-1-910499-39-9 Eyewithin By Mayar Akash	This is the 3rd book of Mayar Akash. The book catalogues the lost paintings by himself.
978-1-910499-37-5 My Dream World By Rashma Mehta	This is the first of Rashma's book filled with her imaginary world of experiences and perception.
978-1-910499-41-2 When You Look Back By Rashma Mehta	This is Rashma's 2nd book filled with her imaginary world of experiences and perception.

ISBN/Titles /Image/Author	Descriptions
978-1-910499-15-3 Anthology One By Penny Authors	This is the first of the Penny Authors Anthologies. Titled, "Anthology One". It is filled with so many different journies.
978-1-910499-17-7 Anthology Two By Penny Authors	This is the second of the Penny Authors Anthologies. Titled, "Anthology Two". It is filled with so many more different journies. Many are the same journies but experienced by different people of various cultures. It is a wonderful place to expand ones horizon.
978-1-910499-29-0 V3 Book of Lived By Penny Authors	This is the third of the Penny Authors Anthologies. Titled, V3 Book of Lived". After the experiences gained from the previous two publications, It became clear that these books were more than average poetry books, These were lived moments recorded. This is the first anthology with the new name. It is a wonderful place to expand ones horizon.
978-1-910499-35-1 V4 Book of Lived By Penny Authors	After the third instalment the momentum for the Penny Authors to come together and share their life journey in so that the reader finds that "missing Jigsaw" piece in their life. If this anthology serves one soul then it has served its purpose. The "V4 Book of Lived is now settling in to its positioning in the world of souls.

ISBN/Titles /Image/Author	Descriptions
978-1-910499-50-4 Anthology Five By Penny Authors	After the fourth instalment the momentum for the Penny Authors to come together and share their life journey in so that the reader finds that "missing Jigsaw" piece in their life. If this anthology serves one soul then it has served its purpose. The "V5 Book of Lived is now settling in to its positioning in the world of souls.
978-1-910499-43-6 My Life Book 1 By Mayar Akashh	Truly fine poetry - The trail and tribulation at a boy forced to be a man far too soon, plunged into a life of emotional turmoil, its truly heart rendering, this book will bring a tear to your eye and a sadness to your heart, does love cancer all? Find out for yourself from this amazing word smith". This is the first book of the author's entire collection of writing since the age of 12 to 43. These books are crammed packed with published and unpublished work, many are unchanged as it was written at first.
978-1-910499-44-3 My Life Book 2 By Mayar Akash	This is the second book of the author's entire collection of writing since the age of 12 to 43. These books are crammed packed with published and unpublished work, many are unchanged as it was written at first.

www.ingramcontent.com/pod-product-compliance
Lightning Source LLC
Chambersburg PA
CBHW060303050426
42448CB00009B/1729